I0815620

This book belongs to:

GREAT CIVILIZATIONS OF PERU

5,000 YEARS OF ANCIENT ANDEAN CULTURES

PICHONCITO

Believe it or not, the disciplines of history, linguistics, and archaeology are constantly evolving, and there are many things we still don't know for certain or about which experts have different opinions. In this book we use the most generally accepted dates and spellings of names—of both people and places—endorsed by our academic advisor, Cecilia Pardo, and by the team of experts at the Museo de Arte de Lima (MALI). For this reason, the information and names presented here may appear slightly differently in other books.

Editor: Adriana Roca
Coordinating Editor: Karina Villalba
Academic Advisor: Cecilia Pardo
Museo de Arte de Lima (MALI) Editorial Committee:
Patricia Villanueva
Julio Rucabado
Research and Composition: Yesenia Silva
Historical Advisor: Ricardo Guerrero
Art Direction: Raquel Tudela
Design, Illustration, and Layout: Melissa Siles
Style Editing: Jorge Cornejo
Translation: Laura Healy
Copy Editor: María Fe Carranza

Edited by © Ediciones Pichoncito S. A. C.
Jr. Santa Rosa 359, Barranco 15063, Lima, Peru
www.pichoncito.pe
R. U. C. 20603234643

First Edition: May 2025
Print Run: 3,000 copies
Printed at Corporate Graphics Commercial
1750 Northway Drive
North Mankato, MN 56003
United States

May 2025
ISBN: 978-612-4450-58-7
Legal Deposit at the National Library of Peru:
n.° 2024-12640

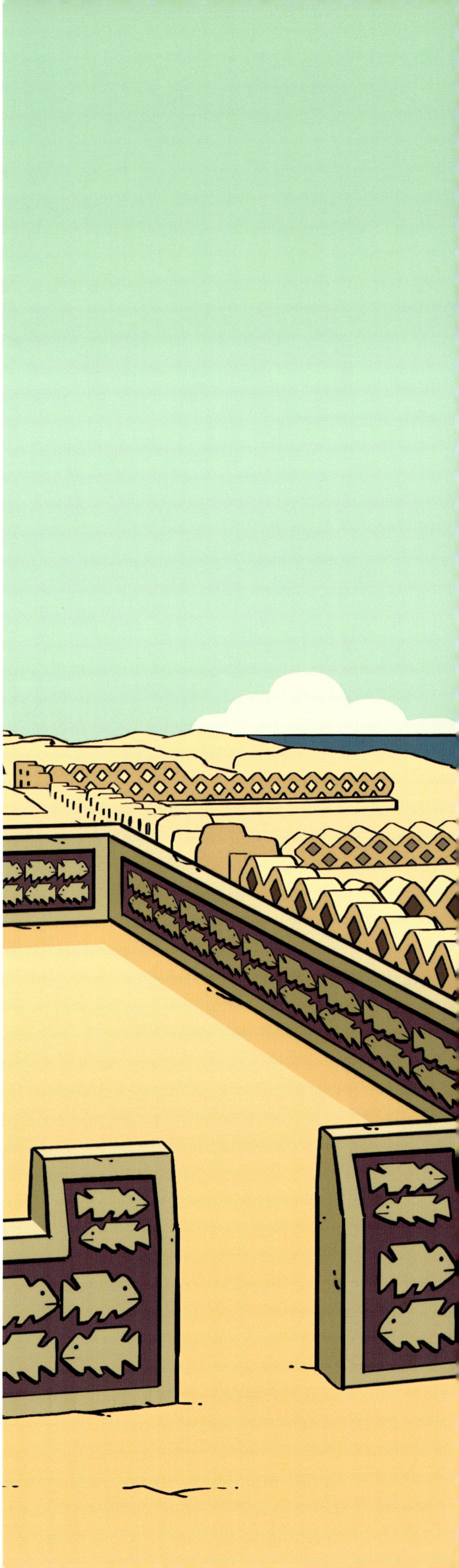

GREAT CIVILIZATIONS OF PERU

5,000 YEARS OF ANCIENT ANDEAN CULTURES

About 16,000 years ago, the first humans made their way from northern America to the territory of modern Peru. They were men, women, and children who fished, gathered fruits, and hunted animals to survive. Thousands of years went by, and these ancient Peruvians learned to cultivate the land, domesticate animals, build villages, and turn their territory's resources into pottery, textiles, and works of gold and silver. They composed songs, narrated myths, and worshipped gods, and in doing so, they forged bonds of fraternity, belonging, and identity.

The American continent's first civilization emerged in the valleys of the Peruvian coast approximately 4,300 years ago—almost three millennia before the ancient Egyptians! Its people built the impressive buildings and pyramids of Caral, which you can visit near Barranca, north of Lima. Since then, numerous cultures have thrived and faded away in Peru, leaving behind extraordinary archaeological remains.

In *Great Civilizations of Peru: 5,000 Years of Ancient Andean Cultures*, you'll uncover the mysteries and traditions behind the art, architecture, and archaeological treasures of the Chavin, Paracas, Nazca, Moche, Recuay, Cajamarca, Lima, Ychsma, Wari, Chancay, Chachapoyas, Chimu—and, of course, the great Incan Empire. Their temples, fine textiles, beautiful ceramic pieces, and great cities connect us to the past and remind us that the creativity, resilience, talent, and fighting spirit of Peruvian men and women date back thousands of years.

It has been an honor for Ediciones Pichoncito to again collaborate with the Museo de Arte de Lima (MALI) and its unmatched team in the co-publication of *Great Civilizations of Peru: 5,000 Years of Ancient Andean Cultures*. We are also deeply grateful to all the specialists who took part in developing this book, without whom we could never have done such a rigorous job. We hope this book will both help Peruvian children gain a thorough understanding of the privilege of being part of this monumental legacy and encourage us all to renew our commitment to its study and preservation.

If Peruvians are the children of the Sun, we hope his luminous dawn shines through on these pages.

Pichoncito Fly Books
Lima, May 2025

Index

How to Use This Book

Prepare to travel back in time and learn how the most extraordinary societies in ancient Peru emerged, who their leaders and rulers were, what life was like in their great cities, and why their legacy has been acknowledged in World Heritage Sites. In *Great Civilizations of Peru: 5,000 Years of Ancient Andean Cultures*, you'll find the answers to these and other questions that capture our interest and imagination to this day.

You can read this book as one long story, from the first humans' arrival on the South American continent to the Incan Empire's conquest of the Andes. But you can also open up to any page and dive into a particular culture or theme—for example, the sacred rituals in the temple of Chavin de Huantar. Revisit these pages as often as you'd like, and you'll discover something new each time.

Below, we'll show you what the symbols in the book mean and teach you how to tell the difference between the various kinds of data and information you'll find inside.

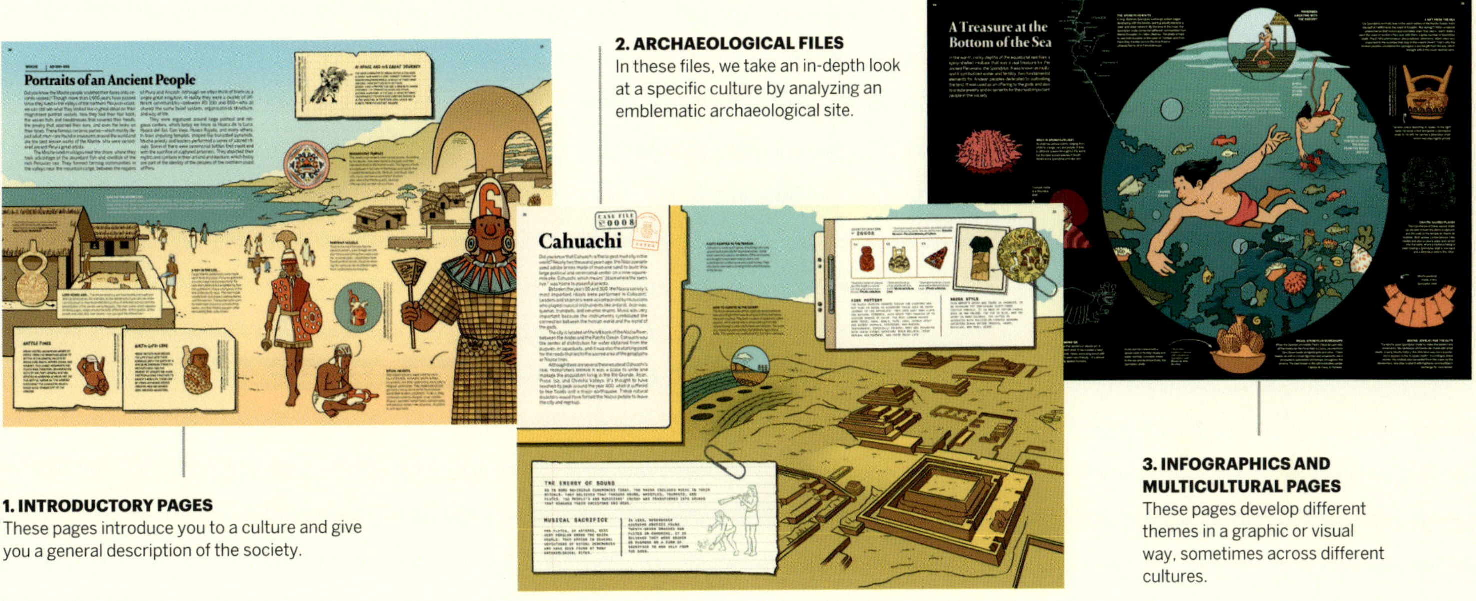

1. INTRODUCTORY PAGES
These pages introduce you to a culture and give you a general description of the society.

2. ARCHAEOLOGICAL FILES
In these files, we take an in-depth look at a specific culture by analyzing an emblematic archaeological site.

3. INFOGRAPHICS AND MULTICULTURAL PAGES
These pages develop different themes in a graphic or visual way, sometimes across different cultures.

4. TIMELINE
While important things were going on in Peru, amazing events were taking place in other parts of the world too! Want to know what they were? Scan this QR code and travel through time to discover what was happening all around the globe!

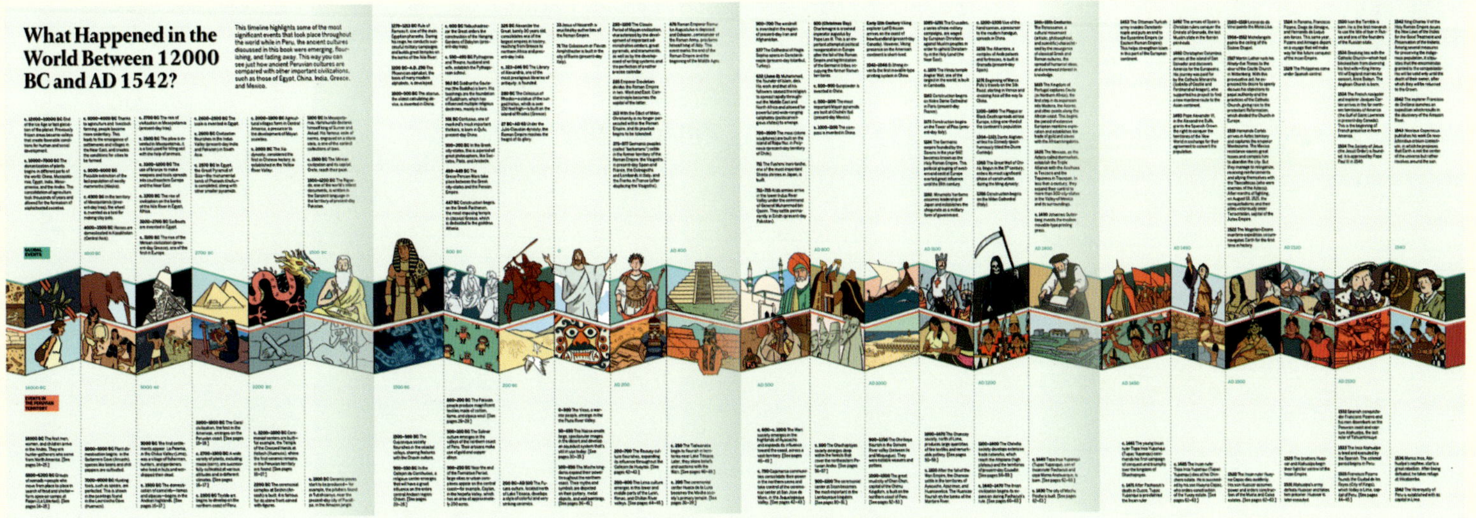

Explorers of the Past

What was life like for the ancient Peruvians? What clothes did they wear? What foods did they eat? Since they left no written record of their history, much of what we know today about Peruvians' ancestors, we owe to archaeology: the science of studying the past by examining the monuments, objects, and organic remains left behind by people from long ago.

When archaeologists find a metal figurine, a tomb, or the remains of a temple, it's like finding a puzzle piece. Part of their job is putting the pieces together to get a sense of what life was like in this region hundreds or even thousands of years ago. Each item left behind by the ancient Peruvians is important to archaeologists. Ceramic vessels, weapons, textiles, murals, mummies—and even garbage! Each one is like a treasure, so they look for them very carefully.

It's not easy to find the remains of an ancient culture. As years go by, natural phenomena like rain and landslides, vegetation, and even new buildings cover up the ancient settlements. Archaeologists dig for clues, but not just anywhere: first, they have to do research to locate the best site and plan out each phase of the work.

The things we know today about ancient Peruvians were first discovered by travelers, explorers, and collectors—and later by archaeologists who wanted to better understand the past. Turn the page to learn who these pioneering researchers were, how their adventures in Peru began, and what amazing things they found in this vast territory.

Are you ready to travel back in time and put together all the pieces of this great puzzle?

INDIANA JONES, LARA CROFT, AND THE SCIENTIFIC METHOD

Unlike the famous archaeologists we see in movies, real archaeologists don't just go searching for relics in exotic locations. Their adventures begin with a question they want to answer, for example, "Who did this tomb belong to?" Next, they dig to find evidence and then analyze it in the laboratory. Finally, they share their findings in articles, books, interviews, conferences, exhibitions—and also films!

THE THREE PRINCIPLES OF ARCHAEOLOGY

THESE ARE THE THREE IDEAS THAT EVERY ARCHAEOLOGIST SHOULD KEEP IN MIND BEFORE, DURING, AND AFTER AN EXCAVATION.

1. **SUPERPOSITION**
NEW ABOVE; OLD BELOW. ACCORDING TO THIS PRINCIPLE, THE LOWER LAYER OR STRATUM WAS FORMED FIRST AND THEREFORE PREDATES THE LAYER OR STRATUM ABOVE IT. THIS IS HOW THE EXCAVATION'S FINDINGS ARE ORGANIZED: FROM THE OLDEST (DEEPER) TO THE MOST RECENT (CLOSER TO THE SURFACE).

2. **ASSOCIATION**
EVERYTHING IS CONNECTED. RESEARCHERS MUST OBSERVE THE RELATIONSHIPS BETWEEN THE DIFFERENT THINGS THEY FIND. FOR EXAMPLE, IF A TOMB CONTAINS JEWELRY OR ADORNMENTS, THEY MAY BE PART OF A PERSON'S GRAVE GOODS.

3. **RECURRENCE**
THERE ARE PATTERNS TO BE FOUND. WHEN RELATIONSHIPS DISCOVERED THROUGH ASSOCIATION ARE REPEATED REGULARLY, A PATTERN OR RULE CAN BE SAID TO EXIST. AN ARCHAEOLOGIST CAN DIFFERENTIATE PARACAS BURIALS FROM THOSE OF OTHER CULTURES BECAUSE EACH HAS ITS OWN RECURRING CHARACTERISTICS, WHICH APPEAR OVER AND OVER AGAIN.

MODERN NAMES

The names by which we know ancient Peruvian cultures are the ones that researchers use, but we don't actually know what the Moche or the Nazca called themselves. These names are like labels that help us organize the past.

* Illustration based on a Moche bottle with a lobed base and depictions of sea lions. **Museo de Arte de Lima.**

* Illustration inspired by a Moche bottle depicting a duck. **Museo de Arte de Lima.**

ARCHAEOLOGIST'S KIT

IN THE FIELD, TOOLS SUCH AS BRUSHES AND TROWELS ARE USED TO DIG FOR CLUES. OTHERS, LIKE MICROSCOPES AND COMPUTERS, ARE CRUCIAL IN THE LABORATORY WHEN IT COMES TIME TO ANALYZE THE FINDINGS. DEPENDING ON THE LOCATION AND THEIR GOALS, ARCHAEOLOGISTS USE DIFFERENT INSTRUMENTS:

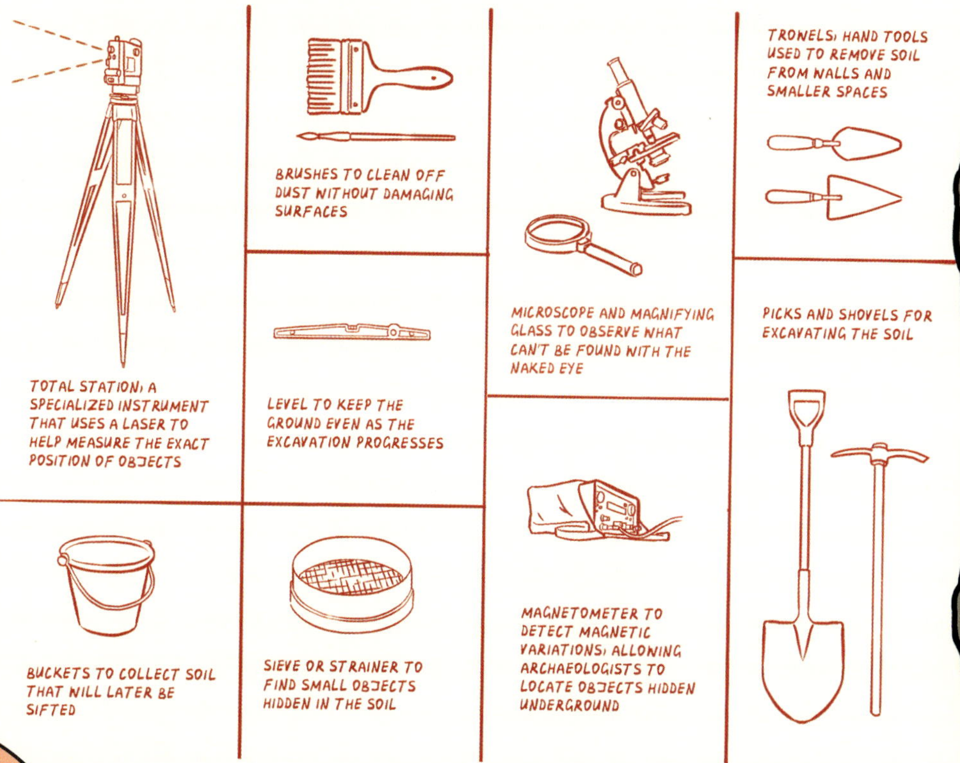

TOTAL STATION, A SPECIALIZED INSTRUMENT THAT USES A LASER TO HELP MEASURE THE EXACT POSITION OF OBJECTS

BRUSHES TO CLEAN OFF DUST WITHOUT DAMAGING SURFACES

LEVEL TO KEEP THE GROUND EVEN AS THE EXCAVATION PROGRESSES

MICROSCOPE AND MAGNIFYING GLASS TO OBSERVE WHAT CAN'T BE FOUND WITH THE NAKED EYE

TROWELS, HAND TOOLS USED TO REMOVE SOIL FROM WALLS AND SMALLER SPACES

PICKS AND SHOVELS FOR EXCAVATING THE SOIL

BUCKETS TO COLLECT SOIL THAT WILL LATER BE SIFTED

SIEVE OR STRAINER TO FIND SMALL OBJECTS HIDDEN IN THE SOIL

MAGNETOMETER TO DETECT MAGNETIC VARIATIONS, ALLOWING ARCHAEOLOGISTS TO LOCATE OBJECTS HIDDEN UNDERGROUND

DRONES
Drones are used to obtain an aerial view of the worksite and its surroundings.

EVERYTHING IN ITS PLACE
It's impossible to excavate without destroying the land, so archaeologists must keep a detailed record of everything they find throughout an excavation. They use a grid to mark the exact location of each piece. They also make drawings, take photographs, and record videos. Later, they use all this information to help recreate an image of the site as they found it.

4

3 1 2

STORYTELLING ANCESTORS

THE PEOPLES OF ANCIENT PERU BELIEVED IN LIFE AFTER DEATH. THAT'S WHY PRE-HISPANIC TOMBS— THOSE FROM BEFORE THE SPANIARDS ARRIVED IN AMERICA—AND EVERYTHING THEY CONTAIN PROVIDE US WITH IMPORTANT INFORMATION ABOUT THE PAST. SINCE THEY REMAINED HIDDEN UNDERGROUND, METAL, STONE AND CERAMIC OBJECTS, AS WELL AS FINE TEXTILES BURIED WITH OR WRAPPING THE BODIES, HAVE BEEN PRESERVED TO THIS DAY.

Scholars of Ancient Peru

As a child, the famous researcher Julio C. Tello enjoyed exploring the sierra on the outskirts of his city, Lima, and playing hide-and-seek among the *chullpas*. "Who lived here?" he wondered, standing in front of these ancient pre-Hispanic tombs, which looked like small houses. When he grew up, Tello set out on more than 30 major archaeological adventures across the northern, central, and southern Andes. These could last weeks, months, or even years! His work to publicize the cultures of ancient Peru was so valuable that—along with Max Uhle—he is today considered the father of Peruvian archaeology.

After the Spaniards arrived in Peru, almost 500 years ago, the search for treasure and riches motivated first conquistadores and then European explorers to travel across the Peruvian territory. But in the mid-19th century, with the arrival of scientists like Wilhelm Reiss and Alphons Stübel, a more organized study of Peru's ancient history began to develop in collaboration with local intellectuals and collectors.

The first chronology of pre-Hispanic cultures was proposed by the German archaeologist Max Uhle. He worked arduously for more than 40 years, gathering field data on the northern coast and sierra; in Ica (where he identified the Nazca culture); on the central coast; and in Cuzco, Arequipa, and Puno. Starting in the 20th century, thanks to Uhle and Tello's contributions, a new generation of professional Peruvian archaeologists emerged, including Rebeca Carrión Cachot, whose studies helped us better understand the role of women and children in ancient Peruvian cultures.

LARCO HOYLE

GUARDIANS OF THE PAST

EARLY COLLECTORS, FROM BOTH PERU AND ABROAD, PLAYED AN IMPORTANT ROLE IN THE DEVELOPMENT OF PERUVIAN ARCHAEOLOGY. OVER THE YEARS, SEVERAL FAMILIES BUILT COLLECTIONS OF OBJECTS AND ARTIFACTS THAT SERVED AS THE BASIS FOR MANY SCIENTIFIC STUDIES AND MUSEUM EXHIBITS. LITTLE BY LITTLE, COLLECTING—WHICH HA[D] ONCE BEEN CONSIDERED A HOBBY—BECAME A PRESTIGIOUS AND HIGHLY VALUED SCIENTI[FIC] PRACTICE.

HUARME[Y]
AD 600
ANCAS[H]

MARIANO EDUARDO DE RIVERO Y USTARIZ
Born in Arequipa in 1798, he was the first director of the Museo de Historia Nacional and the author (in 1840!) of the first book ever published about pre-Hispanic Peru: *Antigüedades peruanas (Peruvian Antiquities)*. His work was translated into German in 1853, and its readers included Wilhelm Reiss, Alphons Stübel, and even Max Uhle.

THE ARCHAEOLOGIST 1822

UNPROTECTED MONUMENTS

IN 1822, THE FIRST GOVERNMENT ORDER PROTECTING PERU'S HISTORICAL AND ARCHAEOLOGICAL MONUMENTS DECLARED THAT ALL OBJECTS FOUND IN HUACAS OR PRE-HISPANIC SITES MUST BE GIVEN TO A NATIONAL MUSEUM. PERUVIANS HAD GAINED THEIR INDEPENDENCE, AND IT WAS URGENT TO REPAIR THE DAMAGE CAUSED BY THREE CENTURIES OF LOOTING AND LOSS. UNFORTUNATELY, THIS LAW EXISTED ONLY ON PAPER AND NEVER ACTUALLY ACHEIVED ITS GOAL.

WILHELM REISS AND ALPHONS STÜBEL

VOLCANOLOGIS[TS]

GERMANY, 1838–1908. GERMANY, 1835–1904

- ARRIVED IN PERU IN 1870 TO STUDY VOLCANOES, BUT BECAME INTERESTED IN THE PRE-HISPANIC PAST AS SOON AS THEY WERE IN THE ANDES.
- IN 1875, PARTICIPATED IN THE EXCAVATION OF THE NECROPOLIS OF ANCON, CONSIDERED TO BE THE FIRST SCIENTIFIC EXCAVATION IN PERU.
- COLLECTED AND STUDIED THE OBJECTS THAT WERE FOUND, WHICH THEY THEN SOLD TO GERMAN MUSEUMS.

Max Uhle
Löben, Annaburg
Deutschland

RELATIVE DATING VS. ABSOLUTE DATING

BOTH ARE IMPORTANT FOR UNDERSTANDING THE HISTORY OF PRE-HISPANIC CULTURES, EACH FOR ITS OWN VIEWS:

RELATIVE	ABSOLUTE
HELPS US UNDERSTAND THE ORDER OF EVENTS AS A SEQUENCE.	ALLOWS US TO PUT SPECIFIC DATES TO THESE EVENTS, LIKE A TIMELINE.
ALLOWS US TO HAVE AN OVERVIEW OF HISTORY AND ITS CHANGES.	EMPLOYS SCIENTIFIC METHODS AND MODERN TECHNIQUES TO OBTAIN ACCURATE RESULTS.
USEFUL FOR UNDERSTANDING COLLABORATION BETWEEN DIFFERENT CULTURES OVER TIME.	USEFUL FOR ESTABLISHING CONNECTIONS BETWEEN HISTORICAL MOMENTS.

DEUTSCHLAND 60

TELLO

PARACAS 200 bBC.

EXCHANGE OF IDEAS
The first research trips were often successful thanks to the help of local people, who lodged the travelers, showed them where to go, or sold them antiquities. But above all, it was the exchange of ideas between Peruvian and foreign intellectuals that made possible the great discoveries of the pre-Columbian past.

IDOL OF PACHACAMAC

* Illustration based on the statue *Idol of Pachacamac*. **Pachacamac Site Museum.**

MAX UHLE — ARCHAEOLOGIST

GERMANY, 1856–1944

- CONDUCTED THE FIRST EXCAVATIONS USING THE STRATIGRAPHIC METHOD AND CAME UP WITH A CHRONOLOGICAL HISTORY OF ANCIENT PERU.
- BECAME INTERESTED IN THE PROTECTION OF ARCHAEOLOGICAL MONUMENTS.
- THE FIRST TO PUBLICIZE THE ORACLE AND PILGRIMAGE CENTER IN PACHACAMAC.

JULIO C. TELLO — DOCTOR, POLITICIAN, ANTHROPOLOGIST

PERU, 1880–1947

- THE FIRST TO PROPOSE THAT PRE-HISPANIC CULTURES ORIGINATED IN THE ANDES. UNTIL THEN, MANY HAD BELIEVED THAT ANDEAN PEOPLE MIGRATED FROM CENTRAL AMERICA.
- CARRIED OUT IMPORTANT EXCAVATIONS AT SITES LIKE CHAVIN DE HUANTAR, PARACAS, AND NAZCA.
- AS A POLITICIAN, FOUGHT TO DEFEND PERU'S HISTORICAL AND ARCHAEOLOGICAL HERITAGE.

REBECA CARRIÓN CACHOT — HISTORIAN

PERU, 1901–GUATEMALA, 1960

- A STUDENT OF JULIO C. TELLO, SHE WAS THE FIRST FEMALE PERUVIAN ARCHAEOLOGIST AND ONE OF THE FIRST FEMALE UNIVERSITY PROFESSORS IN PERU.
- THE FIRST TO USE CARBON-14 DATING ON A FUNERARY BUNDLE FROM THE PARACAS CULTURE.
- DIRECTOR OF THE NATIONAL MUSEUM OF ARCHAEOLOGY AND ANTHROPOLOGY FROM 1947 TO 1955.

RAFAEL LARCO HOYLE — COLLECTOR

PERU, 1901–1966

- IN 1926, FOUNDED THE LARCO MUSEUM AT CHICLIN (LA LIBERTAD) AND, WITH HIS FATHER'S HELP, BUILT A COLLECTION OF 45,000 PIECES FROM ALL OVER PERU. TODAY YOU CAN VISIT HIS COLLECTION AT THE LARCO MUSEUM IN LIMA.
- RESEARCHED AND EXCAVATED VARIOUS SITES ON THE NORTHERN COAST, SUCH AS THE CHICAMA AND VIRU VALLEYS.
- PUBLISHED NUMEROUS ARTICLES AND BOOKS ABOUT HIS FINDINGS.

Living Landscapes

Ancient Peruvian cultures had to use all their creativity and ingenuity to adapt to one of the richest yet most challenging environments on the planet. The first settlers of the Peruvian territory lived in an amazing landscape that shaped their way of life and their understading of the world—from the high peaks of the snow-capped sierra to the arid deserts of the coast, including a great tropical forest and the vast Pacific Ocean.

Cultures of expert fishermen, such as the Moche, flourished in the regions closest to the sea. In the coastal deserts, the Nazca built irrigation systems that allowed them to harvest food from the land. In the high mountain regions, the Tiahuanaco were farmers and herders. And in the tropical forests, where the Chachapoyas lived, they combined fishing, hunting, and agriculture.

Thanks to the Andes Mountains, Peru has an incredible diversity of landscapes and climates: of the 104 ecosystems that exist in the world, Peru has 84. To take advantage of this diversity, the ancient Peruvians created a system known as "vertical control," in which the same group of people could occupy different ecological zones (spaces characterized by their flora and fauna) to obtain a greater variety of resources.

The Peruvians' ancestors believed that all beings and elements in the environment were related to each other and were part of a sacred order. They thought of the landscape as a living being, and this influenced their religious beliefs and practices as well as how they connected with the land, its resources, and each other.

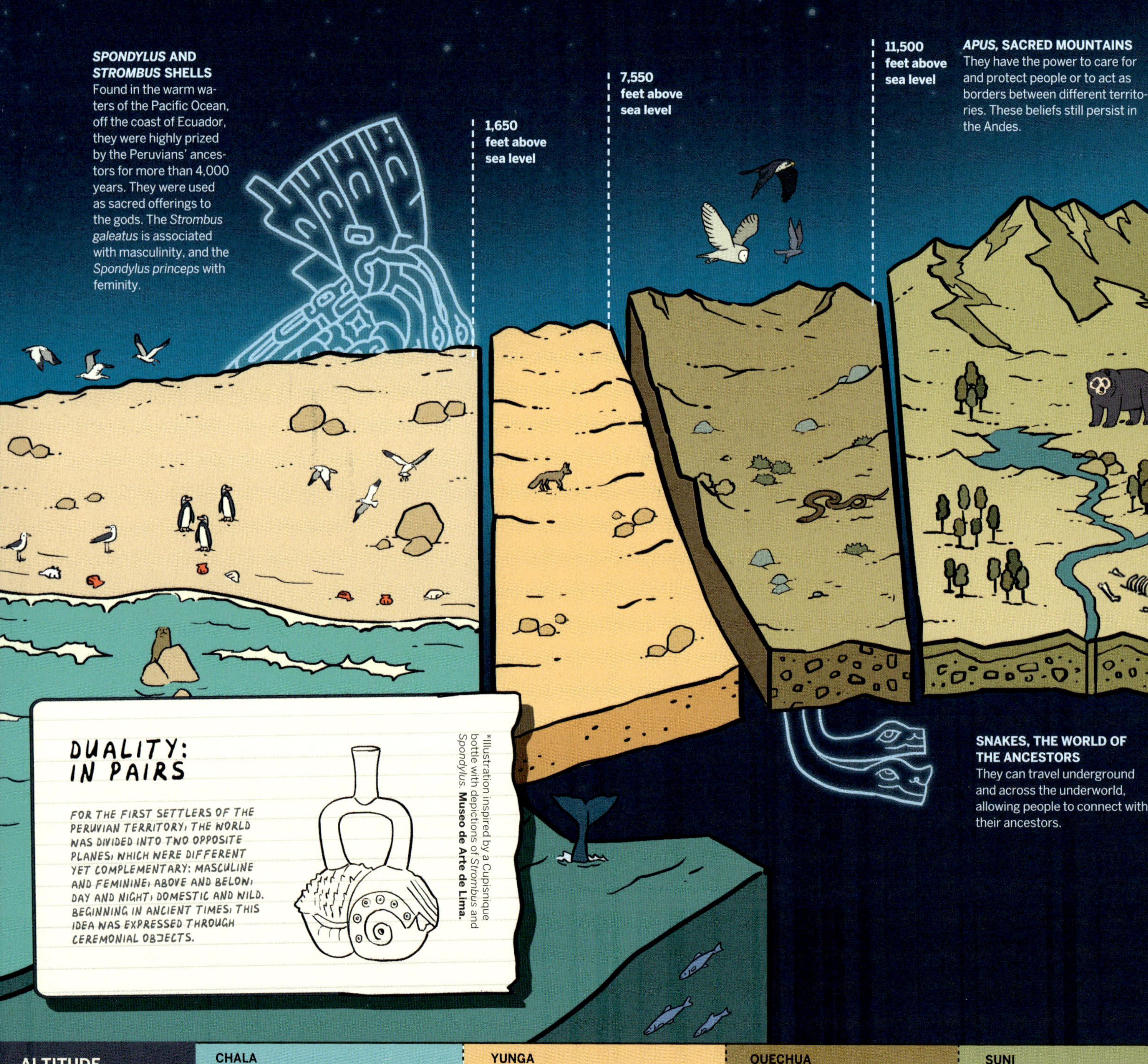

DUALITY: IN PAIRS

FOR THE FIRST SETTLERS OF THE PERUVIAN TERRITORY, THE WORLD WAS DIVIDED INTO TWO OPPOSITE PLANES, WHICH WERE DIFFERENT YET COMPLEMENTARY: MASCULINE AND FEMININE, ABOVE AND BELOW, DAY AND NIGHT, DOMESTIC AND WILD. BEGINNING IN ANCIENT TIMES, THIS IDEA WAS EXPRESSED THROUGH CEREMONIAL OBJECTS.

*Illustration inspired by a Cupisnique bottle with depictions of *Strombus* and *Spondylus*. **Museo de Arte de Lima.**

ALTITUDE LEVELS	CHALA	YUNGA	QUECHUA	SUNI
	0-1,650 feet above sea level	1,650-7,550 feet above sea level	7,550-11,500 feet above sea level	11,500-13,100 feet above sea

CIRCULAR TIME
In ancient Peru, time was understood as a cyclical process, meaning it wasn't seen as something linear, with a beginning (the past) and an end (the future), but rather as a great "spiral" whose phases were repeated in recurring cycles. The past, present, and future weren't separate, but were part of the same cycle. This idea relates to the agricultural cycle, in which each stage (cultivation, planting, and harvesting) repeats year after year.

CATS, THE TERRESTRIAL WORLD
Often jaguars or pumas, they symbolized power and strength. Their tails and fangs appear in depictions of fierce priests, gods, and warriors.

BIRDS, THE NOCTURNAL WORLD
Almost always depicted as eagles or hawks, they symbolize night, war, and darkness. Barn owls and horned owls were also sacred birds.

3,100 eet above ea level

22,200 feet above sea level

7,550 feet above sea level

4,900 feet above sea level

1,300 feet above sea level

WILD DEER
Duality was also expressed in their understanding of sacred animals. In Andean culture, llamas and alpacas symbolize daytime, domestic life, and herding; deer, on the other hand, belong to the world of the ancestors and represent nighttime, wildness, and hunting.

THE CONQUEST'S IMPACT

IN THE MID 16TH CENTURY, THE SPANIARDS' ARRIVAL BROUGHT AN END TO THE ORDER THAT HAD BEEN ESTABLISHED DURING THE INCAN EMPIRE. THE CONQUEST NOT ONLY BROUGHT NEW DISEASES, BUT ALSO DID AWAY WITH ANCIENT LOCAL TRADITIONS. IN THE YEARS THAT FOLLOWED, NEARLY 70 MILLION LIVES WERE LOST IN THE AMERICAS. THE DISAPPEARANCE OF SO MANY PEOPLE, WHO WOULD NO LONGER CULTIVATE THE LAND, DISRUPTED NATURE'S BALANCE. HOWEVER, AGAINST ALL ODDS, MANY ANDEAN TRADITIONS HAVE SURVIVED TO THE PRESENT DAY—FOR EXAMPLE, THE CUSTOM OF USING COCA LEAVES TO GIVE THANKS TO THE GENEROUS PACHAMAMA OR EARTH MOTHER.

PUNA	JANCA	RUPA RUPA	OMAGUA
13,100-15,750 feet above sea level	15,750-22,210 feet above sea level	4,900-7,545 feet above sea level	1,300-4,900 feet above sea level

Peru Before the Conquest

Here are some of the cultures that lived in the territory of present-day Peru before the the great Incan empire of Tahuantisuyo came into power. In this book, you'll find the histories of all the cultures listed here.

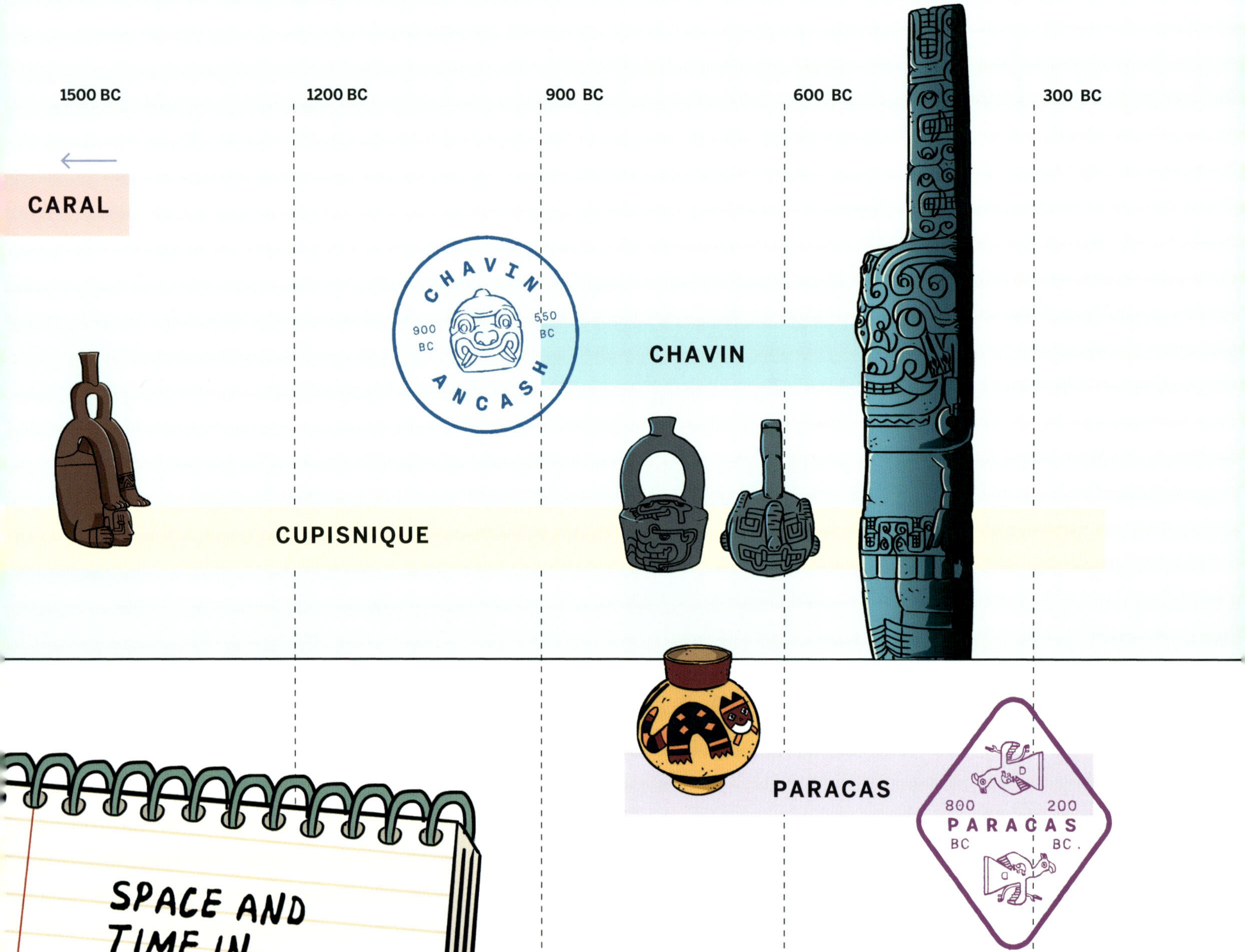

1500 BC | 1200 BC | 900 BC | 600 BC | 300 BC

CARAL

CHAVIN

CHAVIN ANCASH 900 BC 550 BC

CUPISNIQUE

PARACAS

800 BC PARACAS 200 BC

SPACE AND TIME IN PRE-HISPANIC PERU

TO STUDY ANCIENT PERU, RESEARCHERS HAVE PROPOSED DIFFERENT WAYS OF ORGANIZING ITS HISTORY. THERE ARE TWO CHRONOLOGICAL FRAMEWORKS THAT ARE BEST KNOWN AND MOST WIDELY USED BY ARCHAEOLOGISTS: ONE DEVELOPED BY THE AMERICAN JOHN RONE AND ONE PUT FORWARD BY THE PERUVIAN LUIS LUMBRERAS.

STYLISTIC CHRONOLOGY (JOHN H. ROWE, 1964)

It is called this because it divides the past according to the ceramic styles that developed in different eras. "Horizons" are periods in which a single style is predominant across a wide stretch of the Andes. "Intermediate periods" are periods in which several different styles emerge at the same time. This chronology's three great horizons are defined by the styles of the Chavin, Wari, and Inca.

Caral: 2600–1800 BC
Cupisnique: 2200–200 BC
Chavin: 900–550 BC
Paracas: 800–200 BC
Cajamarca: 50 BC–AD 1400
Nazca: AD 50–650
Moche: AD 100–850
Lima: AD 200–600
Recuay: AD 200–700
Tiahuanaco: AD 250–1000
Wari: AD 600–1000
Lambayeque: AD 800–1350
Chachapoyas: AD 900–1470
Chancay: AD 1000–1400
Ychsma: AD 1100–1470
Chimu: AD 1100–1470
Inca: AD 1400–1532

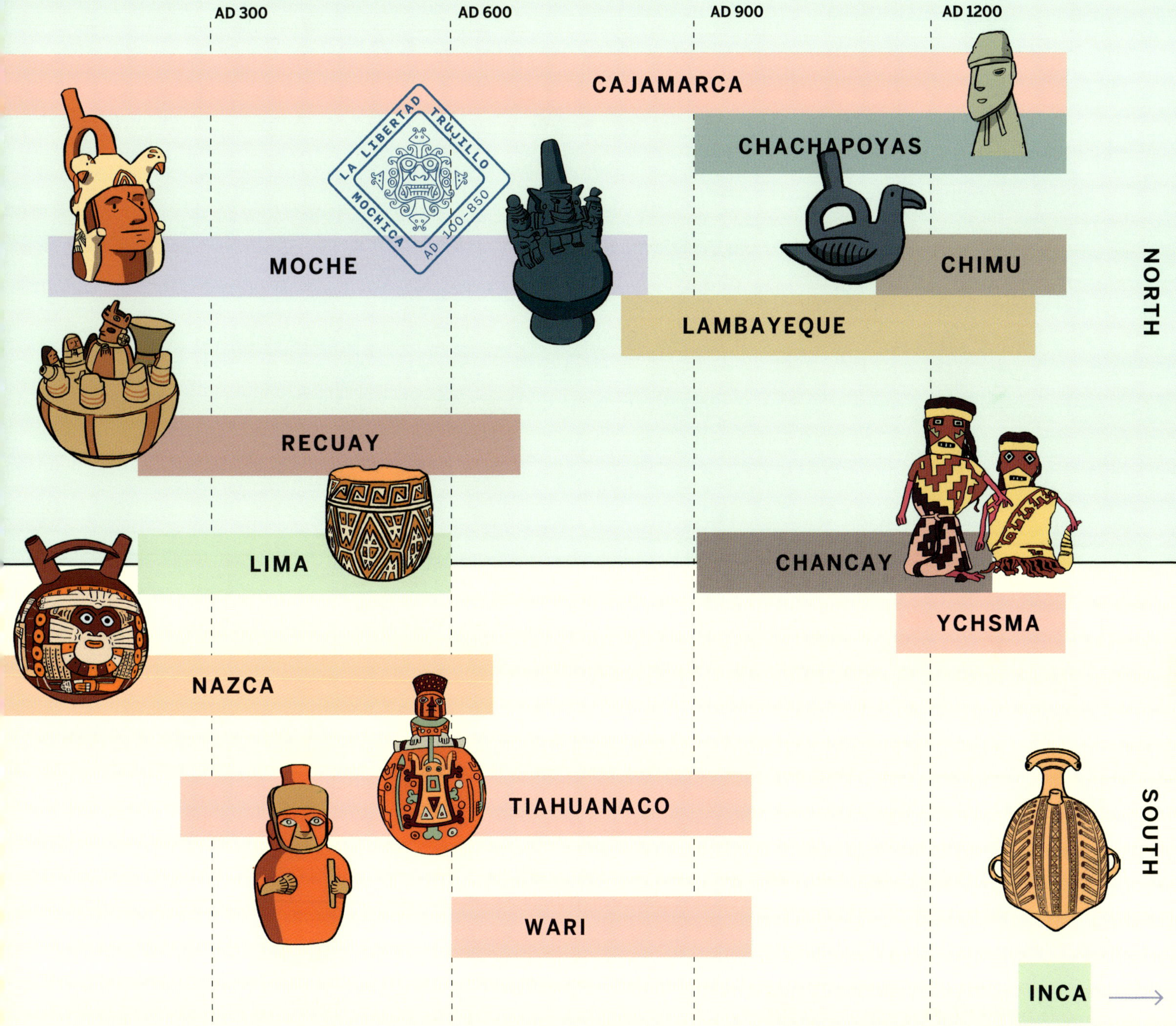

AD 300
AD 600
AD 900
AD 1200

CAJAMARCA
CHACHAPOYAS
LA LIBERTAD TRUJILLO MOCHICA AD 100-850
MOCHE
CHIMU
LAMBAYEQUE
NORTH
RECUAY
LIMA
CHANCAY
YCHSMA
NAZCA
TIAHUANACO
WARI
SOUTH
INCA →

DEVELOPMENTAL CHRONOLOGY (LUIS G. LUMBRERAS, 1969)
It is called this because it organizes the history of ancient societies according to their process of development—that is, the changes researchers find in their way of life (for example, the evolution of their tools or everyday utensils). This chronology is divided into the following periods: Archaic (9000–1500 BC), Formative (1500 BC–AD 200), Regional Development (AD 100–500), Wari (AD 500–900), Regional States (AD 900–1400), and Inca (AD 1400–1532).

First Settlers!

Did you know that one of the last places in the world that humans reached was the central Andes? About 150,000 years ago, groups of hunter-gatherers traveled out of Africa and began to populate different corners of the globe. During the last ice age, which ended about 12,000 years ago, they crossed the Bering Strait (which was frozen and passable) from Siberia, in Asia, to Alaska, in North America—and eventually made it all the way to the Andes. At that time, the mountain range was very different from what it is today: the peaks were completely covered by glaciers!

To survive, the first settlers of the Latin American territory fished, gathered fruits, and hunted Andean animals (like vicuñas, guanacos, and deer) as well as large mammals (like giant sloths and saber-toothed tigers). These ancient settlers had no permanent dwellings. They followed the herds and ate according to the seasons. They slept in caves or straw huts and used animal hides to protect themselves from the cold.

Over time, the glaciers melted, and the climate changed. Some groups were able to settle in areas with better environmental conditions. They began cultivating the land, improved their fishing techniques, and domesticated some animals. Over the course of nearly 10,000 years, ancient men and women adapted themselves to the diverse environments of the desert coast, the inter-Andean valleys, the punas (high plateaus), and the tropical rainforest. They stopped moving from place to place and created the first settlements. And that's how, in ancient Peru, the first civilization in South America began to emerge.

ROCK ART IN LAURICOCHA

In the Huanuco region of Peru, about 12,800 feet above sea level, you can find the Lauricocha Caves, which served as natural refuges for the central sierra's ancient inhabitants. These men and women hunted camelids—their main food source—and painted hunting scenes on the cave walls.

FROM HUNTERS TO FISHERMEN

The oldest evidence of human presence in the Peruvian territory can be found on the northern coast. The Paijan archaeological complex is made up of open-air camps, quarries, and workshops where stone points were made. It is believed that the men and women who lived there transitioned from hunting to catching fish, which became their most important resource.

THE BIRTH OF AGRICULTURE

Some of the world's first farmers lived in the Guitarrero Cave, in the Callejon de Huaylas (Ancash, Peru). Between about 8000 and 5500 BC, plants were cultivated there, including beans, chili peppers, and possibly tubers, like ullucus and ocas.

THE ARCHAIC, A LENGTHY PERIOD

THE ARCHAIC PERIOD ENCOMPASSES THE TIME BETWEEN HUMANS' ARRIVAL IN MODERN-DAY PERU AND THE EMERGENCE OF THE FIRST ANDEAN CIVILIZATIONS. THIS PERIOD CAN BE DIVIDED INTO FOUR PHASES: EARLY ARCHAIC (9000–6500 BC), MIDDLE ARCHAIC (6500–3000 BC), LATE ARCHAIC (3000–2000 BC), AND FINAL ARCHAIC (2000–1500 BC).

The Rise of Civilization

When hunter-gatherers began cultivating the land and domesticating animals, an enormous revolution took place. This didn't happen overnight: it took the ancient settlers of South America about 7,000 years to leave behind their camps and form villages where they could live permanently. They also began building large ceremonial structures. Archaeologists believe the purpose of these structures was to bring together people from different places to worship one or more of the gods they had in common. In their time, the monuments built in northern Peru were the largest on the continent.

Along the coast and the sierra, men and women improved their techniques to make the most of the resources of the sea and the land. Cultivated fields gradually replaced wild plants, and communities started to grow as their harvests could feed a larger number of people. This is when the first leaders emerged. They were in charge of managing daily life. They knew, for example, when it would rain so they could sow and when a drought was approaching so they could store food for survival.

By the year 200 BC, each region was manufacturing textiles, pottery, and metal objects with unique characteristics, and each group of people had its own distinctive art. In addition, the cults surrounding some gods became stronger and spread to a wider territory. As the ancient Peruvians developed new technologies and better managed their living space, they formed increasingly complex societies.

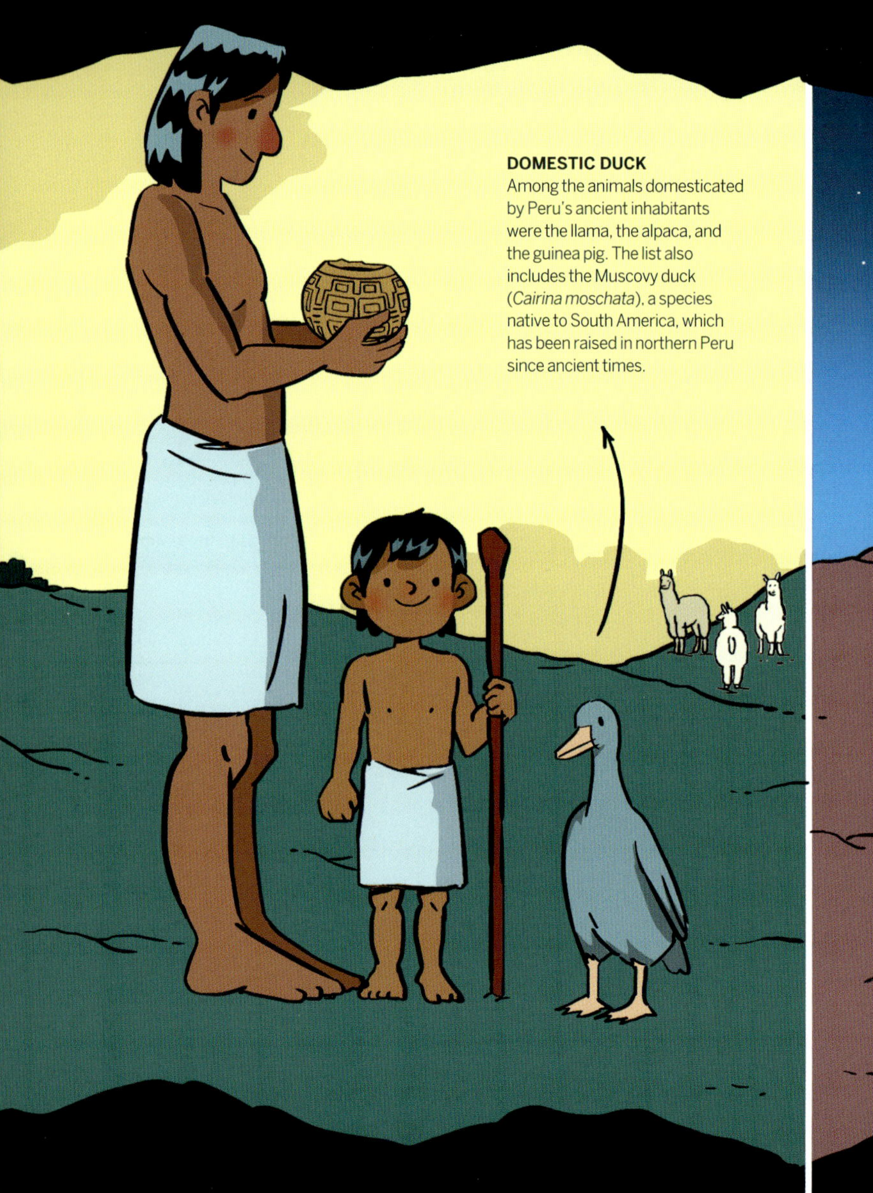

DOMESTIC DUCK
Among the animals domesticated by Peru's ancient inhabitants were the llama, the alpaca, and the guinea pig. The list also includes the Muscovy duck (*Cairina moschata*), a species native to South America, which has been raised in northern Peru since ancient times.

TRADING LUCUMAS FOR PRECIOUS METALS
Residents of different regions traded products according to their communities' needs or as a form of negotiation with other leaders. Those who lived in the jungle or high jungle—a region of dense forests and heavy rainfall, located in the eastern part of the Andes—had access to precious raw materials like jasper, copper, and malachite, which they traded for products from Andean or coastal areas.

1 **NEW TECHNOLOGIES (CIRCA 3500–1700 BC)**
Ancient Peruvian societies invented new technologies and ways of working with the materials they had at hand. For example, they made small human figurines using the technique of firing clay. As offerings, they used gourds decorated with drawings that they engraved using hot embers from the fire, known as pyrographic gourds. (The prefix *pyro* comes from the Greek word for fire!)

2 **ARCHAIC ART (CIRCA 3000–1500 BC)**
Before learning to make pottery, the men and women of ancient Peru produced objects for everyday use using different materials, such as stones, shells, clay, bones, gourds, and wood. During this period, textile development was very important. They used textiles to keep warm, to make bags, to produce blankets for covering themselves as they slept, and even for their journey to the afterlife. Tombs of this period contain mummies covered by beautiful fabrics decorated with repeating designs of diamonds, stripes, and squares, or animals like snakes, birds, and crabs.

THE SIX CRADLES OF CIVILIZATION

THIS NAME IS GIVEN TO THE SIX REGIONS OF THE WORLD WHERE CIVILIZATION EMERGED INDEPENDENTLY, WITHOUT ONE INFLUENCING THE OTHER. ONE CRADLE OF CIVILIZATION IS THE ANDES; THE OTHERS ARE CHINA, INDIA, MESOPOTAMIA, EGYPT, AND MESOAMERICA.

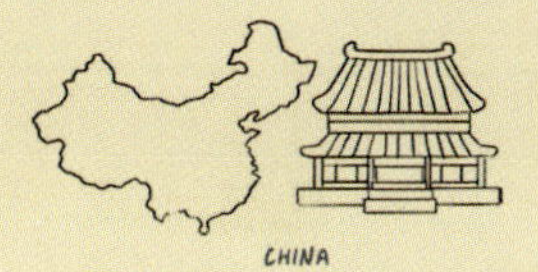

CHINA

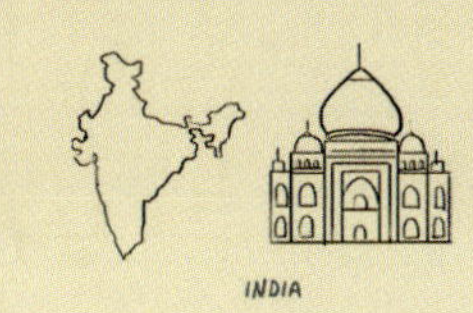

INDIA

MESOPOTAMIA

EGYPT

MESOAMERICA

LARGE STRUCTURES

AROUND 2600 BC, LARGE STRUCTURES WERE BUILT IN VARIOUS REGIONS OF ANCIENT PERU. THESE WERE SOME OF THE MAIN KINDS:

1. PLATFORMS. FLAT-TOPPED STRUCTURES WITH TERRACES BUILT LIKE STAIRS. AT THE TOP, THEY HAD PLACES OF WORSHIP OR ALTARS AND AT THE BOTTOM, ONE OR MORE PLAZAS. IT'S BELIEVED THAT THE LEVELS MARKED DIFFERENT HIERARCHIES DURING RITES OR CEREMONIES: THE LEADERS OR PRIESTS WOULD BE IN THE HIGHEST PARTS AND THE COMMONERS IN THE LOWEST.

2. SUNKEN PLAZAS. RECTANGULAR OR OVAL PLAZAS THAT ARE FOUND BELOW SURFACE LEVEL, LIKE A KIND OF AMPHITHEATER. THEY WERE REACHED BY DESCENDING A FEW STEPS.

3. GROWING BUILDINGS. TEMPLES INCREASED IN SIZE VERY SLOWLY—SOMETIMES OVER A PERIOD OF UP TO 1,000 YEARS! OLDER BUILDINGS WERE PURPOSELY BURIED, AND NEW ALTARS WERE BUILT ON TOP OF THEM, SO THE PLATFORMS GREW TALLER AND TALLER.

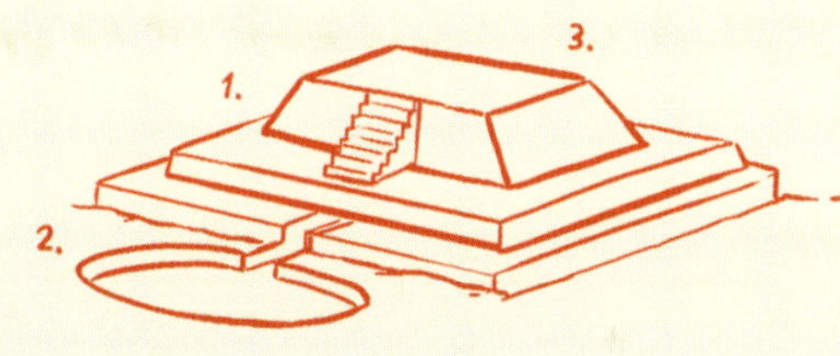

THE TEMPLE OF THE CROSSED HANDS
The Kotosh archaeological site, which can be found to the west of the city of Huanuco in the Peruvian sierra, is home to the famous Temple of the Crossed Hands. This building, discovered by a team of Japanese researchers in 1960, is considered the oldest ritual sanctuary in the Andes (created sometime around 2200–1800 BC) and the first religious monument in the Americas.

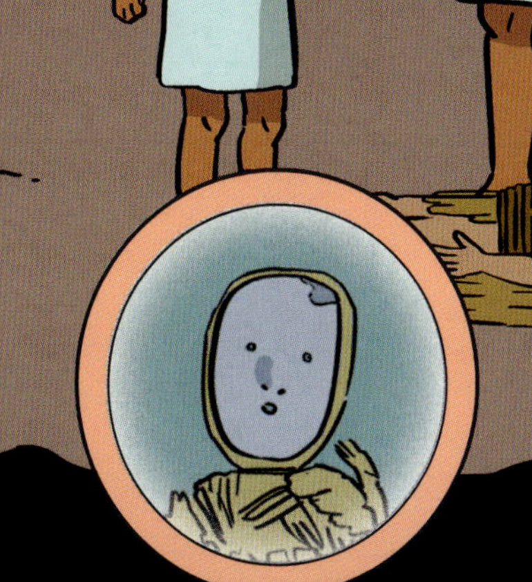

3 CROP DIVERSITY (CIRCA 2700–1500 BC)

The ancient Peruvians domesticated a great variety of plants, which were adapted to different altitudes and climates. Among the most important were the *yuca* (cassava), potato, sweet potato, ullucu, oca, lima bean, common bean, corn, squash, peanut, lucuma, pineapple, papaya, pacay, avocado, granadilla, passion fruit, prickly pear, chili pepper, tobacco, coca, and cotton.

4 THE FIRST MUMMIES

In several ancient cultures, those who were mummified had high status in their communities, such as the Egyptian pharaohs. But, surprisingly, the world's first mummies were mostly children and young people, the sons and daughters of fishermen of the Chinchorro culture, who lived along the coast of the Atacama Desert (which stretches from Ilo, Peru, to Antofagasta, Chile) more than 7,000 years ago—long before the Egyptians!

ARCHAEOLOGICAL CASE FILE

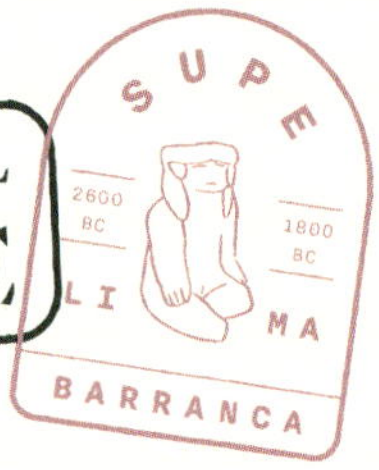

SUPE
2600 BC
1800 BC
LIMA
BARRANCA

Caral

The remains of the oldest civilization in the Americas rise out of a great expanse of sand between the green valleys of the Peruvian coast and the blue waters of the Pacific Ocean. Today, the sacred city of Caral is an imposing monument that has been named a UNESCO World Heritage Site. But about 5,000 years ago, it was the most important administrative and religious center on the northern coast.

Its residents didn't have ceramics, but their scientific and technological advances allowed them to produce a wide variety of objects—like small flutes made from pelican bone—and to build magnificent temples, pyramids, and plazas able to hold large numbers of people. They also traded goods and knowledge with other groups, both near and far. That's how they got *Spondylus* shells, which came from the tropical waters of present-day Ecuador, and sodalite, a gemstone mined in the region of present-day Bolivia.

The city of Caral occupies 66 hectares and is thought to have been designed as a calendar, with buildings oriented toward certain stars. It has 32 structures that were used for public meetings and several clusters of houses: those closest to the center were for the highest ranking leaders. Archaeologists believe that the pyramids of Caral were the first to be built in the Andes.

What secrets does this monumental site hold about the people who lived there between 2600 and 1800 BC? And what was life like back then?

Look through the case file to find out!

WHY DO WE SAY CARAL WAS THE FIRST CIVILIZATION IN THE AMERICAS?

WE SAY THIS BECAUSE ITS RESIDENTS BUILT SETTLEMENTS THAT ALLOWED THEM TO IMPROVE THEIR QUALITY OF LIFE. THEY WERE GOVERNED BY LEADERS WHO ORGANIZED WORK AND RELIGIOUS CEREMONIES. THEY ALSO DEVELOPED IMPORTANT SCIENTIFIC, ARCHITECTURAL, AND ARTISTIC KNOWLEDGE, AND THEY WERE PART OF A NETWORK OF TRADE IN THE VALLEYS OF SUPE, PATIVILCA, AND FORTALEZA (LOCATED IN THE LIMA REGION).

VALLEY SOCIETIES

THE SACRED CITY OF CARAL IS PART OF A GROUP OF 20 SITES WITH LARGE STRUCTURES, ALL LOCATED IN THE SUPE VALLEY. ALL OF THEM HAVE PYRAMID-SHAPED BUILDINGS, CIRCULAR PLAZAS, LARGE RESIDENCES FOR THE MOST IMPORTANT INHABITANTS, AND SIMPLER DWELLINGS FOR THE REST OF THE POPULATION. SOME OF THE OBJECTS FOUND AT THESE SITES INCLUDE STATUETTES, STONE AND GOURD VESSELS, TEXTILES MADE OF COTTON, AND FIRE PITS USED IN RITUAL WORSHIP.

SUPE RIVER
CARAL
LIMA
BANDURRIA
LAS SHICRAS

LIFE IN CARAL

The city's residents were farmers and fishermen, but they also traded goods with other villages, even those located really far away—such as on the beaches of Ecuador or in the valleys of the Andean mountains and jungle. Fishermen used cotton nets to catch various species, like anchovies, mussels, and clams. Farmers in the valley harvested cotton and foods like beans, sweet potatoes, squash, pumpkins, and chili peppers.

WHO'S IN CHARGE OF WHOM?

IN CARAL, EACH "BARRIO" OR *PACHACA* WAS OVERSEEN BY AN AUTHORITY. THE PYRAMID-SHAPED BUILDINGS ARE BELIEVED TO HAVE REPRESENTED THE LINEAGES OR *AYLLUS* THAT MADE UP EACH *PACHACA*. THE *PACHACAS* WERE ORGANIZED INTO DIFFERENT SECTIONS THROUGHOUT THE VALLEY, WHICH WAS DIVIDED INTO TWO HALVES, EACH UNDER THE AUTHORITY OF A LEADER. ABOVE THESE LEADERS WAS THE LORD OF THE VALLEY, OR *HUNO*, WHO RULED OVER THE ENTIRE POPULATION.

HOW WAS THE CITY ORGANIZED?

IN THE CENTRAL PART OF CARAL, THE BUILDINGS WERE ORGANIZED INTO TWO HALVES: UPPER CARAL, WHERE THE PUBLIC BUILDINGS AND LARGEST RESIDENCES WERE LOCATED, AND LOWER CARAL, WHERE THERE WERE SIMPLER, SMALLER STRUCTURES AND DWELLINGS. THE SMALLEST HOUSES WERE CLUSTERED TOGETHER IN THE AREA OUTSIDE THE CITY CENTER, CLOSE TO THE AGRICULTURAL FIELDS.

IMPORTANT FINDS

THE BEST KNOWN FINDS ARE CARVED-BONE FLUTES—PLACED AS OFFERINGS IN ONE OF THE MAIN PYRAMIDS—AND SMALL FIGURINES MADE OF UNFIRED CLAY. BEADS MADE OF *SPONDYLUS*, FISH BONE, AND LOCAL MINERALS LIKE CHRYSOCOLLA (GREENISH IN COLOR) AND BICHLORITE (REDDISH IN COLOR) HAVE ALSO BEEN FOUND.

RUTH SHADY SOLÍS (PERU, 1946)

A PERUVIAN ARCHAEOLOGIST AND EDUCATOR KNOWN AS “THE GUARDIAN OF CARAL,” SHE HAS DEDICATED HERSELF TO RESEARCHING AND PROTECTING THIS ARCHAEOLOGICAL SITE (FORMERLY KNOWN AS “CHUPACIGARRO”) SINCE 1994.

LUXURY BURIAL

THIS GOLD CROWN AND THESE EAR ORNAMENTS WERE FOUND IN THE TOMB OF A MEMBER OF THE ELITE AT THE SITE OF KUNTUR WASI (CAJAMARCA). THE DESIGNS SHOW HUMAN FACES—WITH FELINE FANGS AND SNAKE HAIR! THE EAR ORNAMENTS WITH MOTHER-OF-PEARL INLAYS—WHICH COMES FROM THE COAST—ARE PROOF OF THE LONG-DISTANCE TRADE TAKING PLACE AT THAT TIME.

THE POWER OF THE ELITES

LITTLE BY LITTLE, THE CENTERS WHERE CEREMONIES PAYING TRIBUTE TO THE GODS WERE HELD BECAME VERY IMPORTANT. AND, AS THIS HAPPENED, THOSE IN CHARGE OF PERFORMING THE CEREMONIES ALSO GAINED IMPORTANCE. THAT'S HOW THERE CAME TO BE WHAT'S KNOWN AS A RELIGIOUS ELITE. WHEN ITS MEMBERS DIED, THEY WERE BURIED WITH LUXURY OBJECTS THAT SYMBOLIZED THEIR IMPORTANT POSITION, SUCH AS GOLD CROWNS AND NARIGUERAS (NOSE RINGS), PRECIOUS-STONE BRACELETS, AND METICULOUSLY WORKED CERAMIC VESSELS.

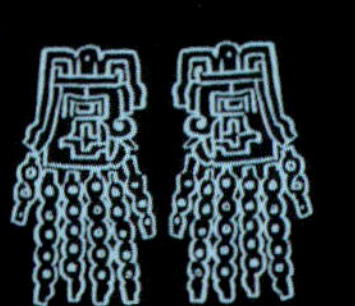

* Illustration based on a crown and ear ornaments from Kuntur Wasi. **Kuntur Wasi Museum.**

CHAVIN, THE GREAT INFLUENCER
Although Chavin de Huantar wasn't the only great ceremonial center of its time, it is the most important and widely studied. It has allowed researchers to learn about the worldview and lives of communities from around 1100 to 500 BC. That's why the religious art of this period is known as "Chavin style." Their beliefs were rendered in textiles and on ceramic vessels that traveled from the ceremonial centers to distant lands.

CHAVIN | 900–550 BC

Fanged Gods

Communities living in different valleys gathered at the ceremonial centers to ask the favor of their gods. These centers popped up throughout the central Andes sometime around 1100 BC. They were smaller than Caral—but there were lots of them! Among the most important were Huaca de los Reyes, in the Moche Valley; Cerro Blanco and Huaca Partida, in the Nepeña Valley; Garagay, in the Rimac Valley; Pacopampa, in the Chotano Valley; Carhua, in the Caral Valley; Kuntur Wasi, in the Jequetepeque mountains; and, the most famous, Chavin de Huantar, in the Mosna Valley.

Around 800 BC, Chavin de Huantar, Kuntur Wasi, and Pacopampa grew in size and power, pushing the smaller centers aside. Their visitors arrived in large pilgrimages from very remote places and, although they belonged to different communities, they shared beliefs, exchanged goods, and practiced the same rituals.

This network of ceremonial centers was in operation for more than 300 years. After it disappeared, new societies emerged in the different regions, such as the Moche, the Nazca, the Lima, and the Recuay. They all had strong identities and their own distinct traits, but they also shared a common past.

SACRED ANIMALS

In ancient Andean times, it was believed that shamans could take on the form and power of some sacred animals, such as the eagle, the feline, the snake, or the caiman. In this form, they could communicate with different creatures from the past and present, who would provide them with important information for the well-being of the community.

WHO WERE THE SHAMANS?

The shamans or priests of ancient Peru were authorities who generally possessed information and knowledge of great importance to their people. For example, they knew how to interpret the position of the stars and the signs of nature to determine the best time for the harvest or to predict the arrival of the rains.

DIVINE ART

The artists of Chavin de Huantar created ceramics, woven cloth, sculptures, and murals, in which they depicted their gods: characters with the features of sacred animals. This style is part of a wider, more-ancient tradition, which appears in different regions of the Andes. On the southern coast, woven fabric with these designs was found in Carhua. In the northern sierra, stone sculptures, ceramic pieces, and gold jewelry were discovered in Kuntur Wasi. And, on the northern coast, reliefs of fanged gods were found on a wall at Huaca Partida.

Chavin de Huantar

CASE FILE
N° 0106

CHAVIN
900 BC
550 BC
ANCASH

Against a backdrop of imposing mountains, under a cloudless, deep-blue sky, stands the temple of Chavin de Huantar—the most powerful and important ceremonial center of its time!

It is located in the Callejon de Conchucos, in the northern sierra of Peru, a strategic location halfway between the coast and the jungle, where the Wacheqsa and Mosna Rivers meet. It is close to the lowlands, with their fertile soil, and to the highlands, where camelids feed on natural grasses. In this mountain valley, 10,500 feet above sea level, the stars shine brilliantly every night, making it possible for shamans to observe the movement of the stars.

Its construction was carried out in several stages and took many centuries. The heart of Chavin de Huantar was the temple, and it is believed that about 3,000 people lived in stone houses in the surrounding area. These families were in charge of manufacturing ritual objects for ceremonies, and it's likely they also helped with the temple's construction. Researchers have discovered that streams were diverted to create underground canals, and long passageways were dug out, forming an actual labyrinth inside.

In Chavin de Huantar, as in other ceremonial centers of the time, the shaman's role was to act as an intermediary between the forces of nature, the gods, and visitors, who were usually authorities from different villages who came from far-off regions to ask the gods for favorable weather and good harvests.

What was the layout of this great temple? Who discovered it? And what happened to Chavin de Huantar in the end?

Find the answers here in this case file!

THE LANZON MONOLITH

THIS ENORMOUS CARVED-GRANITE BLOCK IS ALMOST 15 FEET HIGH AND IS LOCATED IN THE MOST SACRED AND EXCLUSIVE AREA OF CHAVIN DE HUANTAR, WHICH VERY FEW PEOPLE HAD ACCESS TO. IT IS BELIEVED TO REPRESENT THE SUPREME GOD, CHAVIN- AND IT GETS ITS NAME BECAUSE IT IS IN THE SHAPE OF A HUGE LANCE.

THE LANZON GALLERY
THE MOST IMPORTANT MOMENT IN THE CEREMONY WAS ARRIVING AT THE INNER GALLERY OF THE TEMPLE'S CENTER CHAMBER, WHERE THE LANZON WAS LOCATED. SURROUNDED BY TOTAL DARKNESS AND BARELY LIT BY A DIM LIGHT, THE IMPOSING SCULPTURE APPEARED WITH ITS FIERCE FACE, FANGS, SNAKE HAIR, CLAWS, AND UPTURNED EYES.
HEAD ALMOST 3.2 FEET TALL
15 FEET
THE LABYRINTH
CAREFUL, DON'T GET LOST! THE CHOSEN ONES—STILL DISORIENTED AND DIZZY FROM THE EFFECTS OF THE SAN PEDRO CACTUS—HAD TO GO THROUGH A LABYRINTH OF TUNNELS TO REACH THE MOST IMPORTANT GALLERY. THE NOISE OF THE WATER IN THE CANALS WAS SO LOUD THAT IT SOUNDED LIKE A TERRIBLE FELINE'S ROAR.
THE OFFERINGS. Pilgrims entered the underground galleries with altered senses and offered *Spondylus* shells and San Pedro cactus to the gods.
Male Reproductive Organ
THE SUNKEN CIRCULAR PLAZA. The chosen ones prepared themselves here. After eating hallucinogenic substances from plants like the San Pedro cactus, they entered a trance-like state.
SHAMANS OR PRIESTS. They wore masks with feline fangs and snake-like headdresses! Researchers believe they wore ostentatious clothing and accessories with features of sacred animals, which would have shown they had special access to the powers of the gods.

PARACAS | 800–200 BC

Life in the Middle of the Desert

On the coast of Peru, next to one of the richest oceans in the world, the Paracas Peninsula is a vast desert of burning sand. Its name comes from the ancient Peruvian words *para* and *ako*, and it means "sand that falls like rain." Here, hurricane-force winds blow with great intensity, stirring up huge amounts of sand.

Can you imagine what life was like in that arid landscape? The people who lived there 2,500 years ago, known as the Paracas, were able to flourish thanks to their knowledge of fishing, agriculture, and water management. They constructed buildings for ceremonies and rituals, but also houses and workshops where they produced fine textiles and pottery.

They buried their dead in a place surrounded by nature, in the middle of the desert, facing the calm blue waters of the Pacific Ocean. In Paracas tombs, bodies were wrapped in layers of cloth along with various offerings, like ornaments and pieces of pottery, forming a large package called a funerary bundle. The most important and powerful people were buried with more offerings.

The wool and cotton fabrics created by the Paracas have vivid and intense colors. Their clothing and funerary mantles were decorated with geometric figures, plants, animals, people, and gods: supernatural beings with the features of felines, birds, and sea animals.

For many years, researchers studied the Paracas as a distinct society from the Nazca, but recent genetic studies suggest that they were likely the same people at two different moments in history.

SIGNS OF THE PAST

The Nazca lines or geoglyphs—huge figures drawn on the slopes and plains of the desert on the southern coast of Peru—are the best known in the world; however, the Paracas were already practicing this tradition. Large figures made by the Paracas have been discovered from Pisco to the basin of the Rio Grande de Nazca, especially in the area of Palpa. They're found on hillsides and can be seen from far away. Do you think they could have been road signs for ancient Peruvian travelers? What else do you think they could have been for?

ANIMAS ALTAS AND ANIMAS BAJAS

THE LARGE BUILDINGS OF THE ANCIENT ANDEAN CITY OF ANIMAS WEREN'T JUST PART OF THE POLITICAL AND RELIGIOUS CENTER; THERE WERE ALSO AREAS WITH HOUSES AND WORKSHOPS. THE TERRITORY IS DIVIDED INTO TWO PARTS: ANIMAS ALTAS (UPPER ANIMAS) IN THE NORTH AND ANIMAS BAJAS (LOWER ANIMAS) IN THE SOUTH. IT INCLUDES SACRED AREAS, TRANSITIONAL SPACES, DEPOSITS, PLAZAS, AND OTHER SITES LOCATED FARTHER AWAY. ARCHAEOLOGISTS THINK THE PARACAS SOCIETY WAS MADE UP OF SEVERAL DIFFERENT GROUPS THAT SHARED THE SAME RITUALS, TRADITIONS, BELIEFS, AND ORGANIZATION.

CRANIAL TREPANATIONS

The Paracas performed high-risk surgeries on people's skulls (called trepanations) to remove cysts and tumors or to heal combat wounds. These ancient Andean surgeons (Paracas doctors!) used bone awls and tools made of very hard, sharp stone, like obsidian. We know that many of these patients recovered because the bones in their skulls regenerated.

CASE FILE
Nº 0023

800 BC PARACAS 200 BC.

Wari Kayan

On October 25, 1927, in the sweltering heat of the Paracas Bay desert, archaeologist Julio C. Tello's team was excavating when suddenly—they made a surprising discovery! Tello had been determined to find out the origin of some mantles that had been looted from a series of tombs, which is how he ended up on a rocky hill known as Wari Kayan. There, he found an ancient cemetery with more than 400 bodies wrapped in layers of textiles and offerings.

Each of the bundles contained up to 50 objects, including mantles, turbans, tunics, vessels, necklaces, and other accessories. Thanks to the dry, arid climate of the coastal desert, this treasure remained intact for more than 2,000 years—even the delicate fabrics decorated with many different colors of thread.

For the Paracas people, preparing these bundles was a very important ritual because it signified that their deceased relatives were ready to fulfill a new role in the community. They believed the dead had power to influence the weather, the rains, and other forces of nature, and in doing so could improve harvests and the well-being of their descendants.

Unlike Egyptian sarcophagi, which held the deceased forever, Paracas tombs could be opened at certain times to remove the mummies, who were venerated and cared for by their relatives for generations. They would clean the bundles, cover them with new textiles, and add more offerings. When another member of the clan died, they would be placed next to their ancestors to keep each other company.

How did the Paracas people assemble these large bundles? And what's the meaning of the colorful designs on their magnificent mantles?

Find the answers here in this case file!

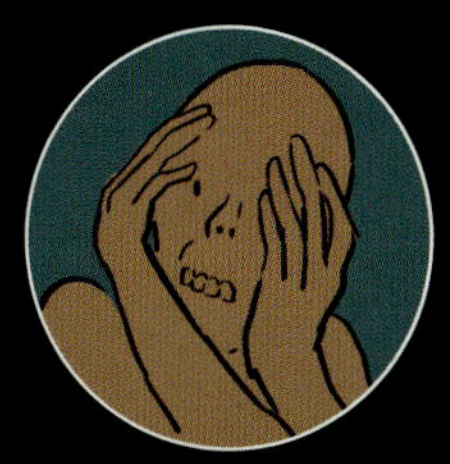

DECORATED ANCESTORS

THE FUNERARY BUNDLES REPRESENTED THE COMMUNITY'S ANCESTORS, SO THEY WERE DRESSED IN CLOTHING AND ADORNED WITH NECKLACES AND *NARIGUERAS* (NOSE RINGS). ON THEIR FALSE HEADS, THEY COULD WEAR HEADBANDS, TURBANS, AND EVEN HAIR.

TEXTILES. Several layers of cloth were used to wrap the mummies and give the bundle a cone shape. They alternated between simple textiles and finely embroidered mantels. They even added a false head by placing a bunch of cloth on the top of the bundle!

OFFERINGS. Gold leaf and small ornaments were placed inside their mouths and in other orifices. Items were also placed around the body, between layers of textiles: new and used clothing, needles, thread, miniature clothing, necklaces, ceramic vessels, fans made of feathers, animal skins, musical instruments, and much more. The quality of the offerings depended on the dead person's status.

MUMMIES. To desiccate (dry out) the bodies, the Paracas people would put them in the sun or bury them in hot sand. Then they put them in a squatting position on top of a deerskin-covered woven basket. The bodies were naked and wore a headdress. Their faces were covered with a mate (dried gourd).

EMBROIDERED STORIES

THE IMAGES EMBROIDERED ON THE FUNERARY MANTLES DEPICT ANIMALS, PRIESTS, AND BEINGS WITH SUPERNATURAL FEATURES. ARCHAEOLOGISTS BELIEVE THESE FIGURES WERE MEANT TO CONVEY MESSAGES ABOUT THE PARACAS PEOPLE'S BELIEFS: THEIR RELATIONSHIP WITH NATURE, THEIR RELIGIOUS PRACTICES, THEIR ANCESTORS, AND THEIR GODS.

GUIDE TO PARACAS ICONOGRAPHY:

TRANSFORMATION
BEINGS WITH HUMAN AND ANIMAL FEATURES REPRESENTED THE MYTHICAL ANCESTORS INTO WHICH THE DEAD WERE TRANSFORMED AFTER BEING WRAPPED IN LAYERS OF TEXTILES AND OFFERINGS.

FERTILITY
FRUITS AND PLANTS—SUCH AS COMMON BEAN AND LIMA BEAN PODS—WERE A REQUEST FOR GOOD CROPS AND MORE ANIMALS. THE BUNDLES THEMSELVES WERE PLACED ON THE GROUND AS IF THEY WERE SEEDS, TO "GERMINATE" AND BE "REBORN" AS ANCESTORS.

SEVERED HEADS
CHARACTERS HOLDING A KNIFE IN ONE HAND AND WHAT APPEARS TO BE A SEVERED HEAD IN THE OTHER APPEAR ON SEVERAL PARACAS MANTLES. SOME RESEARCHERS BELIEVE THEY ARE TROPHY HEADS (FROM ENEMIES DEFEATED IN COMBAT!) OR RITUAL SACRIFICES.

NATIONAL MUSEUM OF ARCHEOLOGY, ANTHROPOLOGY, AND HISTORY OF PERU

WHERE CAN YOU SEE THE MANTLES?

TO FULLY APPRECIATE THE MAGNIFICENT PARACAS TEXTILE ART, YOU CAN VISIT THE MUSEUM OF ARCHAEOLOGY AND ANTHROPOLOGY AT THE UNIVERSIDAD NACIONAL MAYOR DE SAN MARCOS AND THE NATIONAL MUSEUM OF ARCHAEOLOGY, ANTHROPOLOGY, AND HISTORY OF PERU—BOTH IN LIMA—AS WELL AS THE JULIO C. TELLO SITE MUSEUM AND THE ADOLFO BERMUDEZ JENKINS REGIONAL MUSEUM OF ICA.

FABULOUS FUNERARY MANTLES. The Paracas mantles, which today are admired all over the world, were woven on large backstrap looms with threads of cotton and llama, alpaca, or vicuña wool. The intense colors of their embroidery came from natural dyes made of vegetables (e.g., achiote), animals (e.g., cochineal), and minerals (e.g., hematite).

Average Size:
4 x 8 feet

Transforming the Desert

Everyone who flies over them is fascinated by the huge figures drawn upon the pampas (prairies) of Nazca and Palpa, in the desert of the southern coast of Peru. Even though some still believe they were created by aliens (no way!), there's really no mystery to their origin. They were drawn by the Nazca more than 2,000 years ago, and they're so big they can only be seen from the sky. For this region's ancient inhabitants, the pampa was a ritual space: an immense blank canvas on which they created thousands of drawings to honor their gods.

Between 50 BC and AD 650, the Nazca lived in this unique landscape, which is different from other coastal areas. The magnificent desert, located between the Pacific Ocean and the Andes Mountains, was crossed by rivers that flowed down from the Andean mountains and formed oasis-like valleys amidst the sand dunes as well as an underground reservoir of water.

Although the Nazca are best known for their colorful pottery, fine textiles, and famous geoglyphs—the Nazca lines—we now know much more about their worldview and way of life. They built incredible irrigation systems to improve crop production, but they also performed ritual ceremonies on the pampas to mark their ancestors' journey to the afterlife and to ask their gods for the gifts of water and fertility.

By transforming the desert with innovative techniques and great creativity, the Nazca were able to successfully adapt and thrive in one of the most arid regions on the planet.

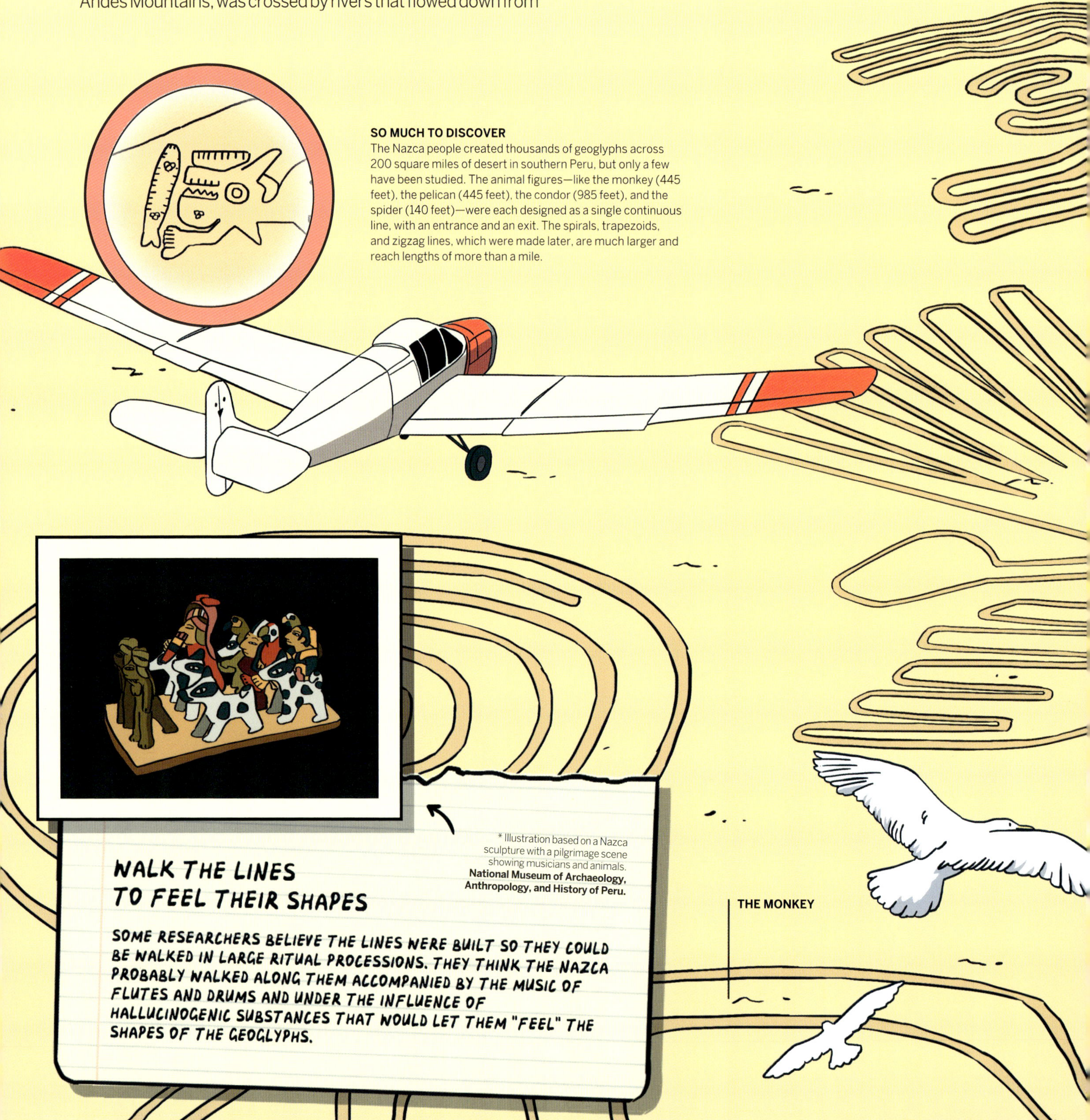

SO MUCH TO DISCOVER

The Nazca people created thousands of geoglyphs across 200 square miles of desert in southern Peru, but only a few have been studied. The animal figures—like the monkey (445 feet), the pelican (445 feet), the condor (985 feet), and the spider (140 feet)—were each designed as a single continuous line, with an entrance and an exit. The spirals, trapezoids, and zigzag lines, which were made later, are much larger and reach lengths of more than a mile.

* Illustration based on a Nazca sculpture with a pilgrimage scene showing musicians and animals. **National Museum of Archaeology, Anthropology, and History of Peru.**

WALK THE LINES TO FEEL THEIR SHAPES

SOME RESEARCHERS BELIEVE THE LINES WERE BUILT SO THEY COULD BE WALKED IN LARGE RITUAL PROCESSIONS. THEY THINK THE NAZCA PROBABLY WALKED ALONG THEM ACCOMPANIED BY THE MUSIC OF FLUTES AND DRUMS AND UNDER THE INFLUENCE OF HALLUCINOGENIC SUBSTANCES THAT WOULD LET THEM "FEEL" THE SHAPES OF THE GEOGLYPHS.

THE MONKEY

HOW WERE THE LINES MADE?

THE REGION'S ANCIENT INHABITANTS CAREFULLY PLANNED THE WORK OF TRACING THE GEOGLYPHS, WHICH TO THIS DAY CAN STILL BE FOUND ON THE NAZCA PAMPAS.

1. THE DESIGN WAS MARKED OFF WITH STONES.
2. THE TOP LAYER OF THE GROUND, MADE OF DARK ROCKS, WAS REMOVED. THIS EXPOSED THE NEXT LAYER OF STONES, WHICH WERE A LIGHTER COLOR.
3. DARK ROCKS WERE PILED UP ON EITHER SIDE OF THE LINE, FORMING A RAISED EDGE.

A. LIGHTER INNER LAYER OF SAND AND GRAVEL.
B. DARKENED SURFACE ROCK (OXIDIZED BY EXPOSURE TO SUNLIGHT).
C. SHADOWS CAST BY RAISED EDGES.

THE SPIDER

THE ARCHAEOLOGIST 2024

NEW FINDINGS

DID YOU KNOW THERE ARE MANY MORE FIGURES HIDING IN PLAIN SIGHT IN THE DESERT OF PERU'S SOUTHERN COAST? MORE THAN 100 YEARS AFTER THEY WERE FIRST STUDIED, THE NAZCA LINES HAVE YET TO REVEAL ALL THEIR SECRETS TO THE WORLD. SINCE 2004, A TEAM OF JAPANESE SCIENTISTS FROM YAMAGATA UNIVERSITY HAS BEEN USING ARTIFICIAL INTELLIGENCE—MORE PRECISELY, A TECHNOLOGY KNOWN AS DEEP LEARNING—AND OTHER TECHNOLOGICAL ADVANCES TO FIND NEW FIGURES ON THE NAZCA PAMPAS. IN A STUDY PRESENTED IN 2016, FOUR NEW GEOGLYPHS WERE UNVEILED: A FIGURE WITH HUMAN FEATURES HOLDING A STICK, A PAIR OF HUMAN OR ANIMAL LEGS, A FISH WITH ITS MOUTH OPEN, AND A BIRD. IMAGINE HOW MANY DRAWINGS AND LINES ARE LEFT TO BE DISCOVERED!

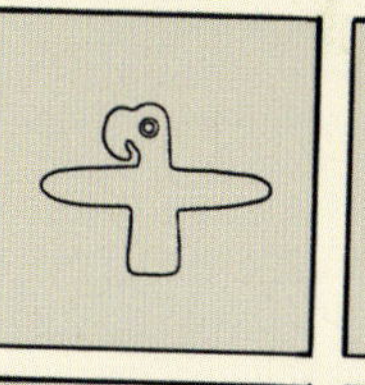

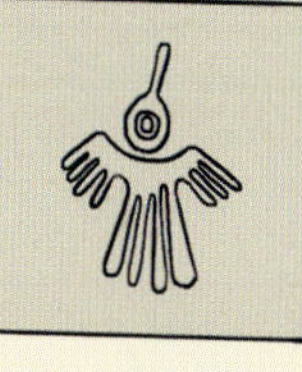

OUT OF THIS WORLD
Since the 1920s, when they were first seen from an airplane, the Nazca geoglyphs have captured the imagination of researchers, travelers, and artists alike. They've also inspired crazy theories among some science fiction fans who think they're a landing strip for spaceships (UFOs).

THE CONDOR

THE MAN

THE LADY OF NAZCA
German mathematician and teacher Maria Reiche dedicated her life to caring for the geoglyphs and studying their shapes: she built a small cabin so she could live near the figures, and for five decades she was their main restorer and guardian. She was born in the city of Dresden, on May 15, 1903, and came to Peru in 1932 to work as governess to the German consul's children. Years later, after making friends with researchers of pre-Hispanic Peru, she became interested in the Nazca culture and began to study the lines. With only a compass, a tape measure, and a couple of measuring instruments (a sextant and, later, a theodolite), she examined nearly 1,000 lines. She would go across the pampas on foot, with a ladder in one hand and a broom in the other, to sweep away the dust and move the stones covering the figures. The Nazca lines only came under UNESCO's protection at the end of 1994. The so-called "Lady of Nazca" died in Lima four years later, in 1998, at the age of 95.

ICA-PERU
AD 50
AD 650
NAZCA

Cahuachi

Did you know that Cahuachi is the largest mud city in the world? Nearly 2,000 years ago, the Nazca people used adobe bricks made of mud and sand to build this large political and ceremonial center on a nine-square-mile site. Cahuachi, which means "place where the seers live", was home to powerful priests.

Between the years 50 and 300, the Nazca society's most important rituals were performed in Cahuachi. Leaders and shamans were accompanied by musicians who played musical instruments like antaras, ocarinas, quenas, trumpets, and ceramic drums. Music was very important because the instruments symbolized the connection between the human world and the world of the gods.

The city is located on the left bank of the Nazca River, between the Andes and the Pacific Ocean. Cahuachi was the center of distribution for water obtained from the *puquios*, or aqueducts, and it was also the starting point for the roads that led to the sacred area of the geoglyphs or Nazca lines.

Although there are several theories about Cahuachi's role, researchers believe it was a place to unite and manage the population living in the Rio Grande, Acari, Pisco, Ica, and Chincha Valleys. It's thought to have reached its peak around the year 400, when it suffered two floods and a major earthquake. These natural disasters would have forced the Nazca people to leave the city and regroup.

A CITY ADAPTED TO THE TERRAIN

Cahuachi is made up of a group of buildings and open spaces built especially for ritual ceremonies. Some areas were also used as cemeteries. Other enclosures are thought to have been used as rooms and workshops for producing ceramics and textiles. Their structures were built according to the natural features of the terrain.

HOW TO SURVIVE IN THE DESERT

The Nazca people used all their ingenuity and creativity to take advantage of the water flowing up to 30 feet below the earth's surface. They built a system of aqueducts called *puquios*, which used gravity to draw water up from the subsoil through a series of channels and trenches. The wate was stored in ponds and then distributed to agricultural fields. This system was so effective that it's still in use today

THE ENERGY OF SOUND

AS IN SOME RELIGIOUS CEREMONIES TODAY, THE NAZCA INCLUDED MUSIC IN THEIR RITUALS. THEY BELIEVED THAT THROUGH DRUMS, WHISTLES, TRUMPETS, AND FLUTES, THE PEOPLE'S AND MUSICIANS' ENERGY WAS TRANSFORMED INTO SOUNDS THAT REACHED THEIR ANCESTORS AND GODS.

MUSICAL SACRIFICE

PAN FLUTES, OR ANTARAS, WERE VERY POPULAR AMONG THE NAZCA PEOPLE: THEY APPEAR IN SEVERAL DEPICTIONS OF RITUAL CEREMONIES AND HAVE BEEN FOUND AT MANY ARCHAEOLOGICAL SITES.

IN 1995, RESEARCHER GIUSEPPE OREFICI FOUND 27 SMASHED PAN FLUTES IN CAHUACHI. IT IS BELIEVED THEY WERE BROKEN ON PURPOSE AS A FORM OF SACRIFICE TO ASK HELP FROM THE GODS.

IDENTIFICATION
Nº 26606

* Illustration based on a Nazca dress decorated with motifs of birds devouring plants, animals, and humans. **Antonini Museum—Peruvian Ministry of Culture.**

01

* Illustration based on a Nazca jug in the shape of a warrior carrying spears and a spear-thrower. **Private collection.**

02

* Illustration based on a Nazca bottle with fish motifs. **Museo de Arte de Lima.**

03

* Illustration based on a Nazca antara decorated with human heads. **Private collection.**

FINE POTTERY

THE NAZCA CREATED CERAMIC PIECES FOR EVERYDAY USE BUT ALSO AS GOODS TO ACCOMPANY THEIR DEAD ON THEIR JOURNEY TO THE AFTERLIFE. THEY USED VERY PURE CLAYS AND NATURAL PIGMENTS, WITH WHICH THEY CREATED UP TO 16 SHADES OF COLOR. THE MOST COMMON PIECES WERE VASES, CUPS, BOWLS, POTS, JUGS, DOUBLE SPOUT AND BRIDGE VESSELS, FIGURINES, AND MUSICAL INSTRUMENTS, ESPECIALLY ANTARAS. MANY ARE DECORATED WITH VIVID SCENES DEPICTING THEIR BELIEFS, THEIR NATURAL ENVIRONMENT, AND THEIR DAILY LIFE.

NAZCA STYLE

THIS WOMEN'S DRESS WAS FOUND IN CAHUACHI, IN AN OFFERING PIT CONTAINING 63 TEXTILE PARCELS. IT IS MADE OF COTTON FABRIC DYED IN TWO COLORS: THE TOP IS BLUE, AND THE SKIRT IS BONE COLORED. THE LATTER IS DECORATED WITH MULTICOLOR PAINTED DESIGNS DEPICTING BIRDS EATING INSECTS, FROGS, REPTILES, AND SMALL BIRDS.

Mythical Beings

They appear on mantles, drums, ornaments, and ceremonial vessels. They have *narigueras*—rings or disks worn in the nose—with feline whiskers (sacred animals that symbolize power and strength). Their mission was to guarantee abundant water and good harvests for their descendants, who had to survive and prosper in the arid desert of the Peruvian coast. They are the Nazca's ancestors: mythical beings who were seen as intermediaries between the human world and that of the gods.

* Illustration based on a Nazca bottle with a motif of the Anthropomorphic Mythical Being. **Museo de Arte de Lima.**

THE MASKED BEING
The principal Nazca god, it is also called the Anthropomorphic Mythical Being—meaning it has a human appearance. It can take on the features of different animals, and it always wears a *nariguera* (nose ring) or mask with feline whiskers and a diadem (crown). Sometimes it also wears a beaded necklace, bracelets, and disk-shaped pendants. Can you find all the faces of people, animals, and mythical creatures that appear in this drawing?

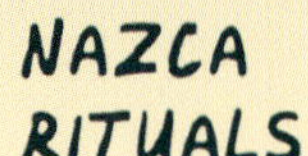

NAZCA RITUALS

THE NAZCA DEPICTED THEIR RITUAL CELEBRATIONS ON OBJECTS LIKE THIS VESSEL. IN THE IMAGES, WE CAN SEE HOW—THROUGH THE USE OF MUSIC AND ACCESSORIES (LIKE HEADDRESSES AND NECKLACES)—THE PRIEST INVOKED THE POWERS OF SACRED ANIMALS TO HELP HIM ON HIS SPIRITUAL JOURNEY. WE ALSO SEE THE SAN PEDRO CACTUS, SOURCE OF A HALLUCINOGENIC SUBSTANCE THAT, ACCORDING TO THE NAZCA, TRANSPORTED THE PRIEST TO THE WORLD OF THE GODS AND THE ANCESTORS.

ILLUSTRATION AND REFERENCE TAKEN FROM THE BOOK *NAZCA*, MUSEO DE ARTE DE LIMA, 2017. DRAWING: CARLA RODRÍGUEZ, REDRAWN FROM PROULX 2006:9, FIG. 1.6.

* Illustration based on a double spout and bridge vessel. **National Museum of Archaeology, Anthropology, and History of Peru. Ministry of Culture.**

1. CAT-WHISKER MASK
It's also called a *nariguera*, mouth mask, or *bigotera*. This last name comes from its large, curved bristles that look like whiskers (*bigotes*), which are decorated with snake and bird heads.

2. DIADEM
Just as European monarchs wear crowns to distinguish themselves from their subjects, mythical beings wear diadems, which are a symbol of their power. Although they appear in many depictions of the Masked Being, researchers have found only two gold diadems that may have been the work of the Nazca.

LIFE AFTER DEATH
The Nazca believed that human beings could transform into ancestors after they died. That's why many of the offerings with which they were buried—ornaments, mantles, and ceramic pieces—were made to accompany the dead on this journey of transformation. The images embroidered on Paracas and Nazca textiles show their deceased turning into mythical beings, wearing diadems and mouth masks, and holding trophy heads.

3. BEADED NECKLACE
A necklace very much like this one, made of 14 trapezoid-shaped *Spondylus* shell beads, was found in the tomb of a priestess in the sacred city of Cahuachi.

4. DISK-SHAPED PENDANTS
Worn in pairs and attached to locks of hair, they appear on both sides of the Masked Being's head.

5. SNAKE-LIKE APPENDAGES
Representing a connection to the world underground, where the ancestors dwell, they protrude from the mythical beings' bodies. They also appear in ceramic and metal statues as supernatural creatures with two heads or with a snake's body and a feline face.

* Illustration based on a sculptural depiction of a two-headed snake. Sculpted and painted. **Antonini Museum—Peruvian Ministry of Culture.**

* Illustration based on a gold ornament in the form of a two-headed serpent with feline faces. **Museo de Arte de Lima.**

MOCHE | AD 100–850

Portraits of an Ancient People

Did you know the Moche people sculpted their faces onto ceramic vessels? Though more than 1,900 years have passed since they lived in the valleys of the northern Peruvian coast, we can still see what they looked like in great detail on their magnificent portrait vessels: how they tied back their hair, the woven hats and headdresses that covered their heads, the jewelry that adorned their ears, and even the looks on their faces. These famous ceramic pieces—which mostly depict adult men—are found in museums around the world and are the best-known works of the Moche, who were considered ancient Peru's great artists.

The Moche lived in villages near the shore, where they took advantage of the abundant fish and shellfish of the rich Peruvian sea. They formed farming communities in the valleys near the mountains, between the regions of Piura and Ancash. Although we often think of them as a single great kingdom, in reality they were a cluster of different communities—between AD 100 and 850—who all shared the same belief system, organizational structure, and way of life.

They were organized around large political and religious centers, which today we know as Huaca de la Luna (Temple of the Moon), Huaca del Sol (Temple of the Sun), Cao Viejo (Old Cao), Huaca Rajada (Cracked Temple), and many others. In their imposing temples, shaped like truncated pyramids, Moche priests and leaders performed a series of sacred rituals. Some of them were ceremonial battles that could end with the sacrifice of captured prisoners. They depicted their myths and symbols in their art and architecture, which today are part of the identity of the peoples of the northern coast of Peru.

AI APAEC AND HIS GREAT JOURNEY

THE MAIN CHARACTER OF MOCHE MYTHS IS THE HERO AI APAEC, WHO MAKES A LONG JOURNEY THROUGH THE ANDEAN-AMAZONIAN WORLD, IN WHICH HE FACES MANY DANGERS: FROM BATTLES WITH MYTHICAL BEINGS—LIKE A PUFFER FISH AND A CRAB WITH HUMAN FEATURES—TO TORRENTIAL RAINS AND OTHER NATURAL DISASTERS. IN THE END, AI APAEC RETURNS TRIUMPHANTLY TO HIS VILLAGE CARRYING SEASHELLS IN ONE HAND AND, IN THE OTHER, COCA LEAVES AND PLANTS FROM THE DISTANT AMAZON.

* Illustration based on "The Journeys of Ai Apaec." Moche ceramic rattle cup. **Larco Museum. Object code: ML018882.**

MAGNIFICENT TEMPLES

The ceremonial centers were sacred spaces. According to the Moche, they were home to the gods and their representatives in the human world. The figures of both are captured in full color in the friezes and murals that covered the temple walls. Festivals and rituals filled with music and dance were held in the temples, where the Moche priests received offerings and carried out sacrifices.

PORTRAIT VESSELS

They're the most famous Moche ceramic vessels, even though we still don't know everything they were used for. In some cases, researchers have found portrait vessels (*huacos*) showing the same person at different ages: from adolescence to maturity.

* Illustration based on a Moche bottle in the shape of a man's head wearing a headdress decorated with birds. **Larco Museum. Object code: ML013572.**

RITUAL OBJECTS

Specialized artisans, supervised by members of the elite, worked to create textiles, ornaments, and other objects that were used in religious ceremonies. They made spectacular garments and accessories for the exclusive use of their leaders and priests. To do so, they combined materials like gold, silver, mother-of-pearl, seashells, cotton fibers, camelid wool, and precious stones—like turquoise, chrysocolla, and lapis lazuli.

Huaca de la Luna

CASE FILE Nº 0103

LA LIBERTAD TRUJILLO MOCHE AD 100-850

An ancient Moche legend tells of two brothers who found a small two-headed snake and took it home to live with them. They didn't know it was a demon and that it would grow bigger and bigger every day until it was the size of a human.

The villagers asked the brothers to get rid of the dangerous snake. Very sadly, the brothers took it to the sea and tricked it into being abandoned. But the animal realized what had happened and started back toward the village. On its way, it fed on everything in its path. It grew so big that one of the neighbors saw it coming from far away and, frightened, warned the others.

The villagers quickly fled to the hillside of the mountain now known as Cerro Blanco. Just as the enormous snake was about to devour them, the hill opened up to let them in and closed again to keep them safe inside. When the danger passed and the villagers came out of the hill, they knew that the mountain god had saved them. That's why, in his honor, they built the temple that is known today as Huaca de la Luna.

If you ever visit this fascinating Moche *huaca* (sacred place), take a good look around! You can still find all kinds of supernatural beings on the walls of its ancient buildings and plazas—including the hungry snake from this story!

CERRO BLANCO
According to legend, the dark-colored line across this mythical mountain is the scar that formed after the ancient Moche's encounter with the ferocious two-headed snake.

HUACA DE LA LUNA
This was the main temple of the Moche society until around the year 700. It's made up of two buildings in the shape of a truncated pyramid: the Old Temple and the New Temple. Only a few chosen people could enter them to worship the gods or to offer their own lives.

*Illustration based on a hanging garment worn by Ai Apaec during the *chacchado* ceremony. **Huacas del Sol and Huaca de la Luna Archaeological Project. Peruvian Ministry of Culture.**

FELINE ATTIRE
This garment is made of supple leather covered by a layer of cotton onto which gold leaf, feathers, and other materials have been sewn to represent a feline pelt. The head is made of wood resin, and the open mouth bares fangs and teeth made of sea shells. The roof of the mouth, tongue, and jaw are made of copper. The eyes are made with inlaid conch shell (the white part) and black stone (the iris). It was found in the Old Temple inside a box, like an offering, and it is depicted on ceramic pieces and drawings, worn by a shaman or victorious warrior.

OLD TEMPLE, AD 50–600
THIS WAS THE MOCHE'S MOST IMPORTANT SACRED BUILDING UNTIL THE SEVENTH CENTURY. IT'S MADE UP OF TWO ADOBE PLATFORMS AND THREE PLAZAS. ITS MAIN STRUCTURE HAS AN IMPRESSIVE FACADE THAT'S 310 FEET LONG BY 80 FEET HIGH, ON WHICH SEVEN BRIGHTLY PAINTED STEPS ARE STILL PRESERVED. ON ITS FACADE ARE DEPICTIONS OF GODS AND MYTHICAL BEINGS, AS WELL AS PRIESTS, DANCERS, AND WARRIORS WHO ACCOMPANIED THE RITES AND CEREMONIES THAT TOOK PLACE IN THE TEMPLE.

NEW TEMPLE, AD 600–850
AROUND THE YEAR 600, GREAT CHANGES TOOK PLACE AMONG THE MOCHE: THE OLD TEMPLE WAS CLOSED AND A NEW, SMALLER AND SIMPLER ONE WAS BUILT NEXT TO IT. THE HIGH-RELIEF FIGURES, WHICH HAD BEEN PAINTED IN MANY COLORS, WERE REPLACED BY OBJECTS AND SYMBOLS ASSOCIATED WITH A FEMALE DIVINITY. THE ERA OF THE WARRIOR-PRIESTS HAD COME TO AN END, AND THE CITY'S INHABITANTS DISCOVERED A NEW FORM OF ORGANIZATION.

HUACA DEL SOL

LEVEL 1. WARRIORS AND PRISONERS: A parade of victorious warriors and their prisoners. The victors bear arms and carry the weapons of the defeated as trophies.

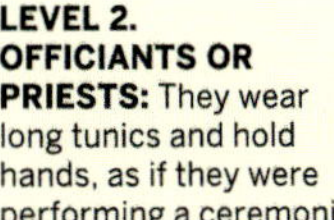

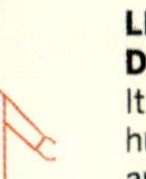

LEVEL 2. OFFICIANTS OR PRIESTS: They wear long tunics and hold hands, as if they were performing a ceremonial dance.

LEVEL 3. DECAPITATING SPIDER: It has features of both a human and a spider. Two arms, holding a knife and a human head, protrude from its abdomen.

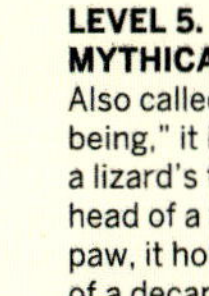

LEVEL 4. MARINE TWIN: It depicts a fisherman carrying two fish hanging by rope.

LEVEL 5. MYTHICAL BEING: Also called "lunar being," it is a feline with a lizard's tail and the head of a fox. In one paw, it holds the head of a decapitated man.

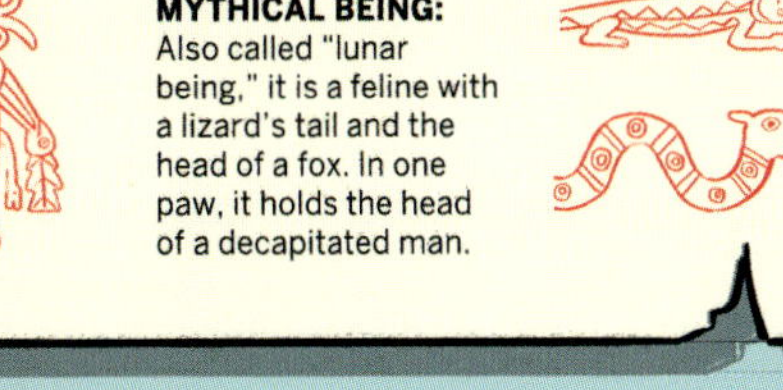

LEVEL 6. DESERT TEGU AND SNAKE: The Peru desert tegu (*cañan*) is a small lizard that lives on the northern coast and was part of the Moche's diet. Along with the snake, it is associated with the river, water, and fertility.

LEVEL 7. MOUNTAIN GOD: Since he's the most important, he occupies the highest step on the facade. He has fangs and wears a diadem. Condor heads appear at the ends of his snake-like appendages.

HUMAN SACRIFICES

In ceremonial plazas, human sacrifices (see pages 40–41) were performed as part of sacred rites. The ceremony began with an agreed-upon ritual combat between warriors. Their objective was not to kill the opponent during the fight, but to obtain his blood and offer it to the gods. The victors took the clothes of the defeated as a reward, and the defeated—naked and tied at the neck with a rope—were taken inside the *huaca* to be sacrificed.

HUACA DEL SOL

IT WAS ONE OF THE MOST IMPRESSIVE ADOBE STRUCTURES IN PRE-HISPANIC AMERICA. IT'S ESTIMATED TO HAVE BEEN 1,130 FEET LONG BY 525 FEET WIDE AND 130 FEET HIGH. THE MOCHE OCCUPIED IT FROM THE VERY BEGINNING, AND IN ITS LAST RENOVATION—AROUND THE YEAR 600—IT GREW IN BOTH SIZE AND IMPORTANCE. UNFORTUNATELY, IT WAS BADLY DAMAGED BY TREASURE HUNTERS DURING THE SEVENTEENTH CENTURY, AND TODAY BARELY A THIRD OF THE ORIGINAL BUILDING REMAINS.

MOCHE | **AD 100–850**

Gods on Earth

Did you know that, for the Moche, human sacrifices were sacred rituals? They could only be carried out by the highest leaders and rulers, as part of an important event that researchers call the Sacrifice Ceremony. In this ritual, the leaders wore the clothing and accessories of Moche gods—like headdresses and nose rings—because they were considered to be representatives of these gods on Earth.

WARRIOR EAGLE
He has the head, wings, and tail of a bird, and he is in charge of delivering the sacrificial cup to the Radiant God. The eagle is a bird that can fly high and approach the sun—just as the Warrior Eagle approaches the Radiant God—but can also dive into the water to fish. That's why it's seen as being able to unite both worlds: the wet and the dry!

THE RITUAL BATTLE
It began with warriors armed with clubs and shields and ready for combat. They would fight hand-to-hand, almost always in pairs, with the goal of deafeating and caputuring their opponent. Once the battle was over, the defeated would be taken prisoner and stripped of their clothing and weapons. Then, they would be taken to the temple to begin the Sacrifice Ceremony, in which the priests and priestesses received their blood as an offering.

RADIANT GOD
Also called Warrior God, he is the god of the dry season and was associated with the Sun. In this scene, he receives an offering of a cup containing the prisoners' blood. He wears a helmet with a crescent-shaped ornament and snakes fanning out like rays. He is accompanied by a spotted dog.

FELINE CARRIED IN A LITTER

* Illustration based on a depiction of the Sacrifice Ceremony on stirrup-handled bottle with a neck. **Staatliches Museum für Völkerkunde, Munich.**

REALITY OR MYTH?
For many years, researchers have wondered whether these scenes depicted on vessels and murals actually happened in real life. Is it possible that these mythical stories were recreated by real priests and prisoners? Recent archaeological findings indicate that yes, it's quite possible.
In the tomb of the Lord of Sipan, elements were found that associate him with the Radiant God. In the tomb of the Owl Priest of Sipan, insignia like those of the Warrior Eagle were found. And in San José de Moro, two women were buried with headdresses and cups very much like those of the Moon Goddess.

THE LORD OF SIPAN
He was an important Moche ruler who would have exercised power in the region now known as Lambayeque. The Peruvian archaeologist Walter Alva found his tomb in 1987, in the truncated pyramid at Huaca Rajada, where other chiefs of the Moche elite were also buried. In the Lord of Sipan's mausoleum, objects of great ritual value were discovered, such as gold and turquoise earrings, mythical characters made out of metal, and gold and silver necklaces depicting peanuts. In the tomb, he was accompanied by some of those in his service as well as by guardians who would care for him on his journey to the world of the dead.

THE LEGEND OF AI APAEC

WHEN THE SUN DISAPPEARS INTO THE SEA AND LURKING DARKNESS THREATENS THE WORLD, THE HERO AI APAEC COMES TO THE RESCUE. HE FLIES UP THE MOUNTAIN ON A BIRD AND THEN HEADS TOWARD THE SEA. THERE, HE BEGINS A LONG JOURNEY THAT BRINGS HIM FACE TO FACE WITH ALL KINDS OF FANTASTIC CREATURES—INCLUDING A PUFFER FISH AND A BEING THAT IS HALF-CRAB, HALF-HUMAN. FINALLY, IN THE DEPTHS OF THE SEA, HE MEETS THE MOST POWERFUL BEING AND FIGHTS HIM. AI APAEC DIES AFTER THE BATTLE, BUT HE IS TRANSFORMED INTO AN ANCESTOR AND REBORN FROM THE DEEP, BRINGING BACK THE SUN.

THE HERO'S POWERS

IN EACH OF HIS ENCOUNTERS, AI APAEC CAPTURES HIS OPPONENTS' STRENGTH OR ESSENCE SO HE CAN USE THEIR POWERS FOR THE BENEFIT OF THE PEOPLE. FOR EXAMPLE, WHEN HE REACHES THE HIGH JUNGLE, BEYOND THE ANDES, HE TRADES WITH THE CHACCHADORES—PEOPLE WHO PERFORM THE RITUAL OF CHEWING COCA WHEN THE RAINS BEGIN—EXCHANGING STROMBUS SHELL TRUMPETS FOR COCA LEAVES. WHEN THE RAINS PASS, AI APAEC LOOKS UP, CLASPS HIS HANDS TOGETHER, AND SEES A LARGE TWO-HEADED SNAKE APPEAR IN THE SKY. HE THEN PLACES THE SNAKE AROUND HIS WAIST AND TAKES FROM IT THE POWER TO MAKE RAIN AND FILL THE RIVERS.

MOON GODDESS
She wears a tunic, and the ends of her braids end in snake heads, no less! She holds a cup in her hands and walks toward the Radiant God.

AI APAEC?
Some researchers believe that this character represents the hero Ai Apaec. Others think it is the Milky Way God—counterpart to the Radiant God and deity of the night sky, the stars, and the humid or rainy season. On his forehead, he wears a headdress with a drawing of a feline.

A TWO-HEADED SNAKE DIVIDING THE DRAWING INTO TWO PARTS: THE HEAVENS AND THE EARTH

MALE CHARACTER COLLECTING A PRISONER'S BLOOD IN A VESSEL

FEMALE CHARACTER COLLECTING A PRISONER'S BLOOD IN A VESSEL

GROUP OF WEAPONS

THE PRIESTESSES OF SAN JOSE DE MORO
Starting in the year 600, the priestesses secured their hold on power in the Jequetepeque Valley. They were in charge of rituals and were associated with a very powerful female divinity: the Moon Goddess. It is believed that they played an important role as mediators between different communities in the area. Since their discovery in 1991 by archaeologists Luis Jaime Castillo and Christopher Donnan, ten tombs of priestesses have been found in the San Jose de Moro cemetery.

THE LADY OF CAO
The tomb of this Moche ruler, also known as the Señora de Cao, was discovered in 2005 by archaeologist Régulo Franco in the Huaca Cao Viejo, part of the El Brujo Archaeological Complex in the Chicama Valley. Her forearms, ankles, and fingers were covered with tattoos of snakes, spiders, and geometric designs, which symbolized the world of the ancestors, rain, and fertility. Did you know that her accessories and symbols of power are very similar to those of the mythical hero Ai Apaec? In particular, the headdress with a feline image. According to researchers, it's possible that she represented the great Moche hero during rituals.

* Illustration based on a Recuay *paccha* (ritual vessel) with a scene of an officiant with acolytes. **Museo de Arte de Lima.**

CAJAMARCA | 50 BC–AD 1470 RECUAY | AD 200–700

Neighbors in the Sierra

Have you heard of the Andean dragon? It's a mythical animal with features of a feline, a bird, and a snake. It's also called the Recuay dragon because it was the main god of the ancient people of that name. The Recuay were the Moche's neighbors, and they flourished in the sierra, at the foot of the Cordillera Blanca and its highest peak—the imposing, snow-capped Huascaran. Their fortified villages were surrounded by walls and moats to protect against intruders and were close to their potato, corn, and quinoa fields and the pastures where their camelid herds grazed.

The Recuay interacted with the Moche in many ways. Both peoples believed in and worshipped the Andean dragon, which is why its image appears on ceremonial vessels, bottles, and murals. But, as happens with even the best of neighbors, they didn't always get on well, and their interactions sometimes ended in conflict and fighting. The Recuay warriors—with their highland clothing and weapons—appear in some Moche ceramic pieces as captured and defeated enemies.

Beginning in the year 850, the Moche lost influence on the northern coast. At the same time, another group of neighbors—the Cajamarca—established dominance and took control of the ceremonial center at San Jose de Moro, in the Jequetepeque Valley. Archaeologists believe that this group exerted great influence over the entire northern sierra region until around the year 700 and that they carried on with their customs until the arrival of the Incas.

A VERY SPECIAL DRAGON

It has many names: Andean dragon, Recuay dragon, crested animal, lunar animal, and even feline, dog, or fox rampant (because it's always on the prowl and ready to attack). It doesn't look much like the European dragons of fairy tales, but it does resemble other supernatural beings of ancient America—for example, the feathered serpent of the Olmec or the god Quetzalcóatl of the Aztecs. Like them, the Andean dragon is a mixture of several sacred animals: it has the large, round eyes of an owl, the long snout of a fangless crocodile, and an ever-extended tongue. Its claws look like those of some birds, and its body, long and sinuous, is like that of a snake. This mythological character has been depicted in ancient Peruvian art—both on the coast and in the sierra—since more than 4,000 years ago.

* Illustration based on a piece of Recuay pottery depicting a site protected by high walls and towers. **Fowler Museum at UCLA.**

HOW DID THE RECUAY LIVE?

THE RECUAY LIVED IN COMPOUNDS PROTECTED BY WALLS UP TO 50 FEET HIGH, WHICH THEY BUILT ON HILLTOPS OR IN OTHER HARD-TO-REACH PLACES. THESE FORTIFIED SETTLEMENTS WERE VERY IMPORTANT BECAUSE THEY OFFERED PROTECTION TO MEMBERS OF THE COMMUNITY WHO LIVED IN THE SURROUNDING AREA, AND IT'S POSSIBLE THEY WERE HOME TO THE RECUAY ELITE. THE COMPOUNDS HAD CEREMONIAL COURTYARDS, WHERE LARGE BANQUETS WERE HELD, AND TOWER-LIKE STRUCTURES THAT SERVED AS TOMBS FOR THEIR ANCESTORS.

ENEMY OF MINE

IN THE COMBAT SCENES DEPICTED BY THE MOCHE, ONE NOTICES WARRIORS FROM OTHER VILLAGES, POSSIBLY THEIR RECUAY NEIGHBORS. IN THESE SCENES, THE ARMED MOCHE APPEAR WITH THEIR CHARACTERISTIC CLOTHING AND CLUBS (WITH MUSHROOM-LIKE HEADS), AND THEY FACE ENEMIES WITH PAINTED FACES, WHO HAVE BEARDS, MUSTACHES, AND LOCKS OF HAIR PARTIALLY COVERING THEIR FOREHEADS, AS WELL AS CAPES AND HEADDRESSES THAT RESEARCHERS HAVE LINKED TO THE RECUAY.

LIMA | AD 200–600 YCHSMA | AD 1100–1470

Ancient Lima

When Francisco Pizarro founded the city of Lima in 1535, he must have been shocked to find a region of very fertile valleys right in the middle of the coastal desert of the Andes. A sophisticated network of irrigation canals spanned its rivers, wetlands, and hills, having been built by the societies who'd lived there many centuries before the Spaniards arrived. The ancient inhabitants of these valleys transformed the desert and took advantage of the Peruvian sea's many resources in order to survive and flourish at different moments throughout history.

Between the years 200 and 750, the central coast's most important society was the one now known as Lima. Its inhabitants built large administrative centers, like the one at the Maranga Complex, to oversee the communities in the valley. They grew crops like corn, beans, peanuts, squash, and custard apple. They lived on the coast during the same period as the Moche and Nazca and, like them, had a special relationship with the sea. Some researchers even believe they were expert divers because they ate deepwater fish, like achovies and tuna.

Around the year 1100, almost three centuries after the end of the Lima culture, the lordship of Ychsma appeared. It was

one of the primary kingdoms in the area until the Incas arrived in 1472. The Ychsma consolidated their power on the coast by expanding the sanctuary of Pachacamac, one of the most prominent oracles in the Andes. (You can go see it!)

The impressive city we now call the Maranga Complex—which is illustrated on these pages—was first occupied by the Lima, who made it their main administrative and ceremonial center. Next, it was occupied by the Maranga community (who were subjects of the Ychsma lordship). Finally, the Incas arrived. They expanded some areas, built walls, and adapted its buildings to meet the needs of the Empire.

FEATHER HAT

DID YOU KNOW THAT, AMONG THE YCHSMA, THESE HEADDRESSES WERE WORN ONLY BY CHIEFS AND OTHER POWERFUL PEOPLE? THE ONE YOU SEE HERE, KNOWN AS THE "TOCADO PURUCHUCO"—OR "PURUCHUCO HEADDRESS"—WAS FOUND ON A MUMMY. IT HAS A STUNNING MULTICOLORED PLUME AND A FISH DESIGN ON THE BACK. IT IS MADE OF CAMELID WOOL AND A VARIETY OF FEATHERS: THE BROWN ONES ARE DUCK, THE WHITE ONES ARE HERON, THE PINK ONES ARE FLAMINGO, AND THE IRIDESCENT ONES ARE MACAW.

WHAT IS A HUACA?

HUACA GARAGAY

HUACA IS A QUECHUA WORD MEANING "SACRED." IN THE TIME OF THE INCAS, A *HUACA* COULD BE A PLACE, LIKE A TEMPLE, A HILL, A LAKE, OR A CAVE. IT COULD ALSO BE AN OBJECT, LIKE A STONE OR AN IDOL, OR EVEN CERTAIN PEOPLE, LIKE THE INCA RULER OR HIS MUMMY. ANY PERSON, PLACE, OR THING THAT THE ANCIENT PERUVIANS CONSIDERED SACRED COULD BE A *HUACA*.

HUACA CRUZ BLANCA

A COLOSSAL JOB

CAN YOU IMAGINE HOW MANY PEOPLE AND HOURS OF WORK IT MUST HAVE TAKEN TO BUILD THIS AMAZING CITY? DEFINITELY A LOT! FOR RESEARCHERS, THE MARANGA COMPLEX REFLECTS THE LIMA SOCIETY AT ITS BEST. THEY BELIEVE THE ELITES MUST HAVE BEEN INCREDIBLY POWERFUL AND EFFICIENT IN ORDER TO MANAGE THE POPULATION AND COMPLETE CONSTRUCTION OF THIS MONUMENTAL SITE.

The First Empire

Did you know there was a great empire in the South American Andes before the Incas? About 1,400 years ago, a warrior people called the Wari emerged from the heart of the region now known as Ayacucho, in the southern highlands of Peru, and crossed the mountains to conquer new territories.

At its peak, the Wari State was able to successfully integrate different communities within an enormous territory that stretched from Cajamarca in the north to Moquegua in the south. In the regions they controlled, the Wari built monumental administrative centers such as Huiracochapampa (La Libertad), Cerro Baul (Moquegua), and Piquillacta (Cuzco). Each of them had a similar, easily recognizable design, with large roofed buildings and wide ceremonial plazas.

Wari leaders weren't just interested in expanding their borders and their architecture; they also spread their way of seeing and understanding the world. On their pottery and textiles—which they could easily transport—they created special images and designs to explain their beliefs. This is how they imposed their rituals and customs on people throughout their enormous territory. Because of this, researchers often compare them to other famous empires of ancient history, like the Romans and the Incas.

Around the year 1000—about four centuries after they emerged—the rise of the Wari in the Andes came to an end, but their influence carried on even during the era of Tahuantinsuyo. For example, the first *quipus*, having been adapted to the needs of the Incan State, were a legacy of this great empire.

WARI FASHION
This ceremonial shirt or *uncu*—produced using the tapestry technique—was worn by a funerary bundle, perhaps in order to indicate the person's identity or the position he held during his lifetime. A character is repeated again and again within the vertical stripes on its design. Can you see him? He is a divine being that looks like a human but has feline and camelid features. He is on his side. In one hand, he has a staff or cane; in the other, he holds a prisoner by the hair. This type of design, which is repeated to form a larger composition, is typical of the Wari style.

*Illustration inspired by a four-cornered Wari hat. **Museo de Arte de Lima.**

FOUR-CORNERED HATS
They are square shaped and their upper corners end in points or loose threads. Researchers believe that they were worn by leaders and authorities and that they even indicated which community a person belonged to. They were also worn by another great people of the Peruvian altiplano (high plateau): the Tiahuanaco.

TEXTILE ART: TECHNOLOGY WITH STYLE

WARI TEXTILES ARE FAMOUS FOR THEIR HIGH QUALITY AND THEIR COLORFUL, SOMETIMES VERY-SOPHISTICATED DESIGNS. ACCORDING TO RESEARCHERS, IT'S POSSIBLE THAT ONLY A FEW MEMBERS OF THE ELITE WERE ABLE TO UNDERSTAND AND REPRODUCE THEM. THE WARI DEVELOPED SPECIAL TECHNIQUES THAT ALLOWED THEM TO COME UP WITH UNIQUE STYLES; THE MOST COMMONLY USED WERE TAPESTRY, TIE-DYE, AND PATCHWORK.

TAPESTRY
A TIGHTLY WOVEN TEXTILE THAT COMBINES DIFFERENT COLORED YARNS. TO ACHIEVE A FIRM, YET SOFT AND FLEXIBLE CLOTH, THE WARI COMBINED DIFFERENT FIBERS (COTTON, VICUÑA WOOL) AND USED VERY FINE THREAD, AS LITTLE AS 0.004 INCHES THICK. THIS TECHNIQUE ALLOWED THEM TO PRODUCE ONE OF THEIR TYPICAL GARMENTS: THE SHIRT OR *UNCU*.

TIE-DYE
A TECHNIQUE THAT INVOLVES TYING KNOTS IN THE FABRIC BEFORE DYEING IT SO THAT SOME PARTS REMAIN DYE-FREE. WHEN THE FABRIC DRIES AND THE KNOTS ARE UNTIED, DESIGNS ARE REVEALED.

PATCHWORK
THE JOINING OF SMALL, PREVIOUSLY DYED FABRIC SCRAPS TO CREATE A LARGER COMPOSITION. THIS TECHNIQUE WAS USED TO MAKE THE *UNCUS* WORN BY WARI WARRIORS, WHICH HAD A CHECKERBOARD PATTERN.

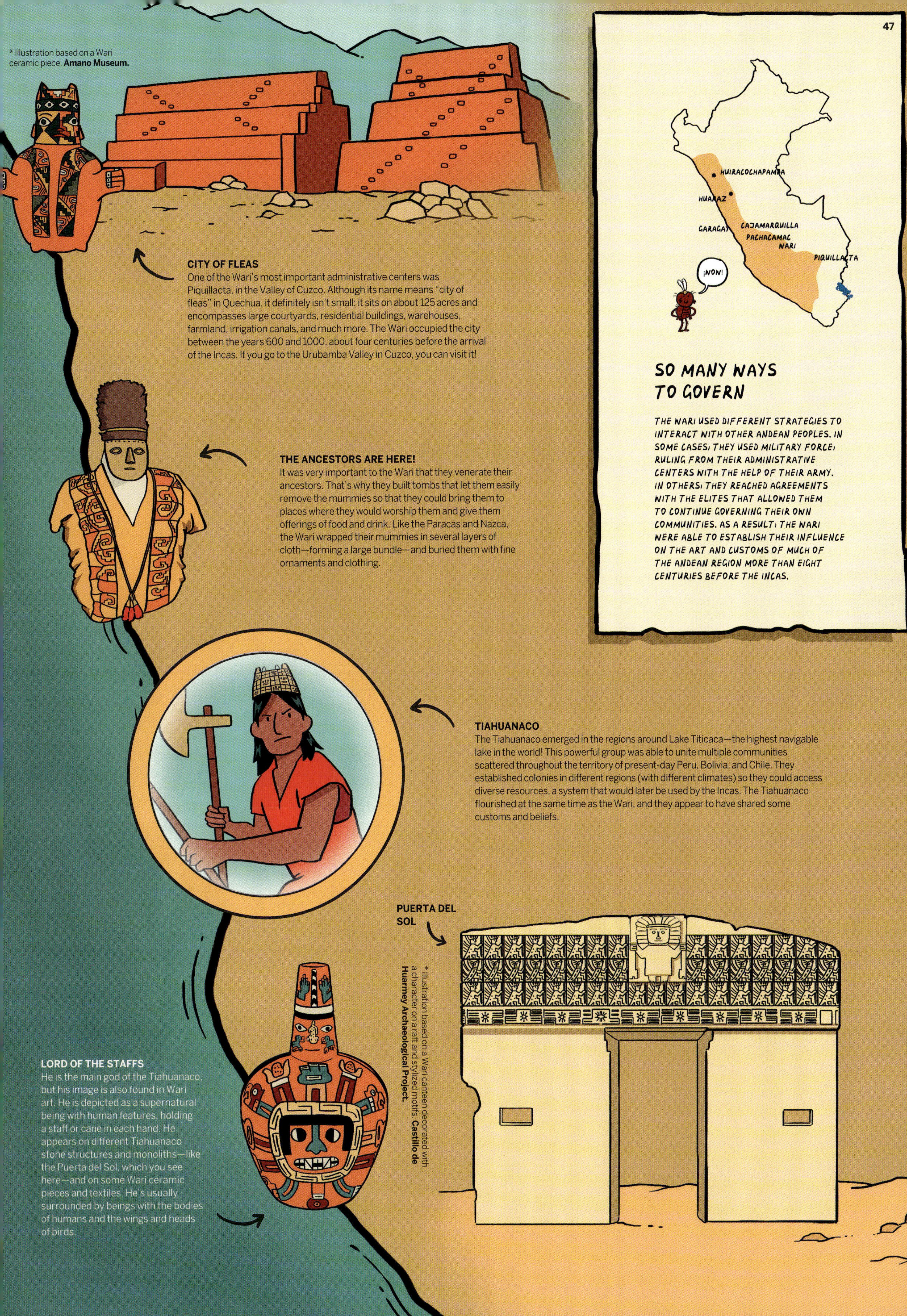

* Illustration based on a Wari ceramic piece. **Amano Museum.**

CITY OF FLEAS

One of the Wari's most important administrative centers was Piquillacta, in the Valley of Cuzco. Although its name means "city of fleas" in Quechua, it definitely isn't small: it sits on about 125 acres and encompasses large courtyards, residential buildings, warehouses, farmland, irrigation canals, and much more. The Wari occupied the city between the years 600 and 1000, about four centuries before the arrival of the Incas. If you go to the Urubamba Valley in Cuzco, you can visit it!

SO MANY WAYS TO GOVERN

THE WARI USED DIFFERENT STRATEGIES TO INTERACT WITH OTHER ANDEAN PEOPLES. IN SOME CASES, THEY USED MILITARY FORCE, RULING FROM THEIR ADMINISTRATIVE CENTERS WITH THE HELP OF THEIR ARMY. IN OTHERS, THEY REACHED AGREEMENTS WITH THE ELITES THAT ALLOWED THEM TO CONTINUE GOVERNING THEIR OWN COMMUNITIES. AS A RESULT, THE WARI WERE ABLE TO ESTABLISH THEIR INFLUENCE ON THE ART AND CUSTOMS OF MUCH OF THE ANDEAN REGION MORE THAN EIGHT CENTURIES BEFORE THE INCAS.

THE ANCESTORS ARE HERE!

It was very important to the Wari that they venerate their ancestors. That's why they built tombs that let them easily remove the mummies so that they could bring them to places where they would worship them and give them offerings of food and drink. Like the Paracas and Nazca, the Wari wrapped their mummies in several layers of cloth—forming a large bundle—and buried them with fine ornaments and clothing.

TIAHUANACO

The Tiahuanaco emerged in the regions around Lake Titicaca—the highest navigable lake in the world! This powerful group was able to unite multiple communities scattered throughout the territory of present-day Peru, Bolivia, and Chile. They established colonies in different regions (with different climates) so they could access diverse resources, a system that would later be used by the Incas. The Tiahuanaco flourished at the same time as the Wari, and they appear to have shared some customs and beliefs.

PUERTA DEL SOL

* Illustration based on a Wari canteen decorated with a character on a raft and stylized motifs. **Castillo de Huarmey Archaeological Project.**

LORD OF THE STAFFS

He is the main god of the Tiahuanaco, but his image is also found in Wari art. He is depicted as a supernatural being with human features, holding a staff or cane in each hand. He appears on different Tiahuanaco stone structures and monoliths—like the Puerta del Sol, which you see here—and on some Wari ceramic pieces and textiles. He's usually surrounded by beings with the bodies of humans and the wings and heads of birds.

Castillo de Huarmey

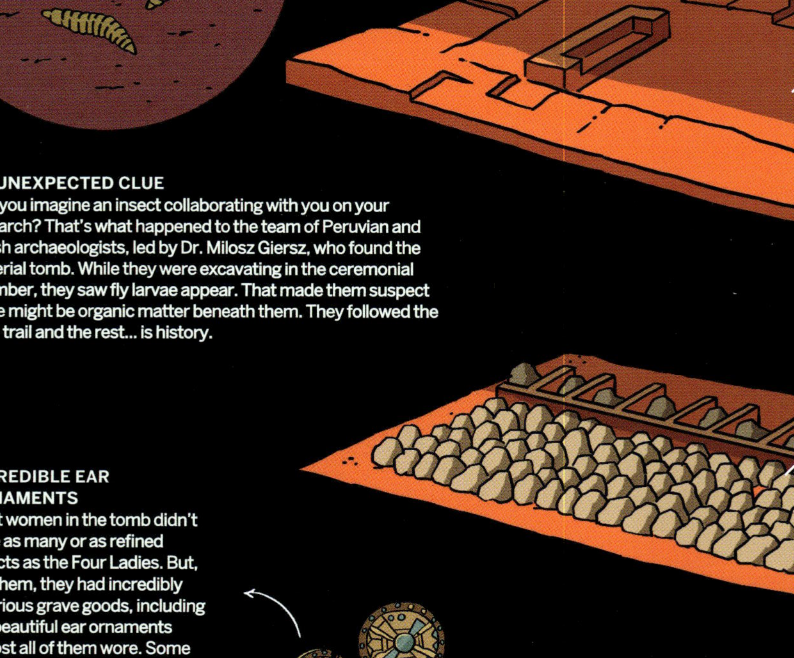

Did you know that, for more than 1,000 years, a magnificent treasure remained hidden inside an important Wari complex known as Castillo de Huarmey? *Huaqueros*—thieves who steal pre-Hispanic artifacts—had plundered the site for decades, leaving it almost in ruins. That's why archaeologists who'd been working in the area for more than 10 years were so surprised to discover a large, intact imperial tomb.

Inside, there were 63 mummies—almost all of them women—and more than 1,300 luxury objects made of gold, silver, bronze, bone, carved wood, ceramic, and textile. Among the objects meant to accompany this group of Wari queens and princesses on their journey to the afterlife were jewelry (ear ornaments, necklaces, pectorals, pendants, rings, brooches), weapons (axes, knives), accessories (small containers for storing lime, rattles, whistles), weaving instruments (looms, needles, spoons with natural dyes), and different kinds of vessels (pitchers, bottles, canteens, cups, and bowls).

But who were these women? Researchers believe they were in charge of making the finest textiles, which had a very special value: only the best-quality garments were given as gifts to the gods or to powerful families. Or they may have been a group of prestigious ladies who performed important ceremonies in their community: along with the weaving tools, archaeologists found spectacular ear ornaments, which were only used by top leaders, as well as ceremonial vessels that were used to serve *chicha* (corn beer) at major events.

Like other powerful leaders—for example, the Lady of Cao and the priestesses of San Jose de Moro (Moche) or the Lady of Chornancap (Lambayeque)—the women of Castillo de Huarmey were buried with honors, as befitted the most-important and highest-ranking figures in ancient Peru.

Turn the Book

SECRETS OF THE IMPERIAL MAUSOLEUM
Fortunately, the mummies and their grave goods were well hidden deep inside a mausoleum whose surface had been damaged by the *huaqueros* long ago. Beneath a ceremonial chamber, archaeologists discovered a layer of adobe bricks in the shape of a trapezoid that looked like a seal. When they removed the bricks, they found layers of earth, more bricks, and rock debris that had been used as fill. They had to carefully remove everything to find the famous ladies of Castillo de Huarmey.

* Illustrations based on a selection of pieces showing the stylistic diversity of the vessels found at Castillo de Huarmey. Sculpted, molded, and painted. Dimensions vary. **Castillo de Huarmey Archaeological Research Project. Peruvian Ministry of Culture.**

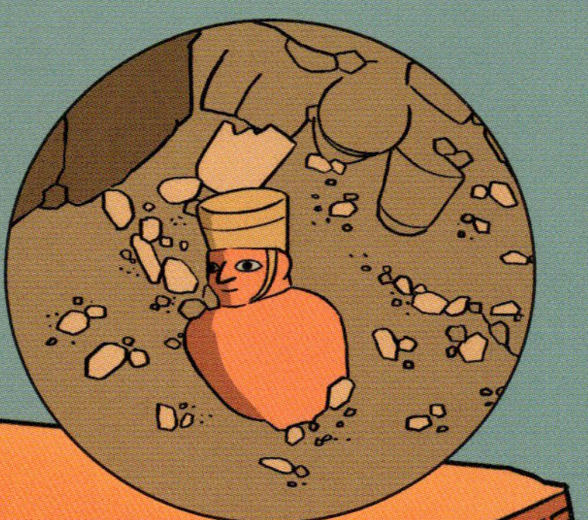

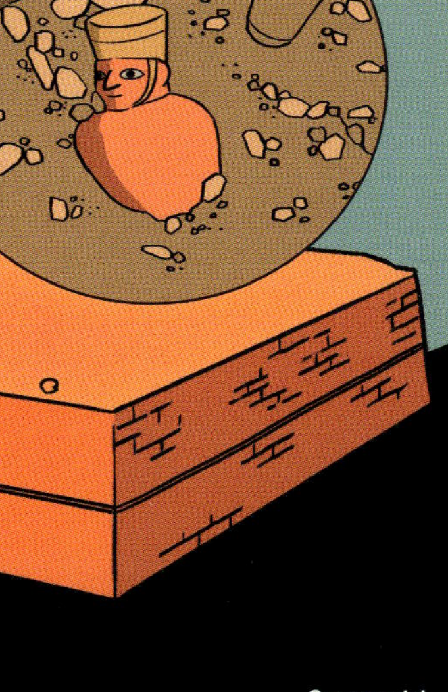

Castillo de Huarmey

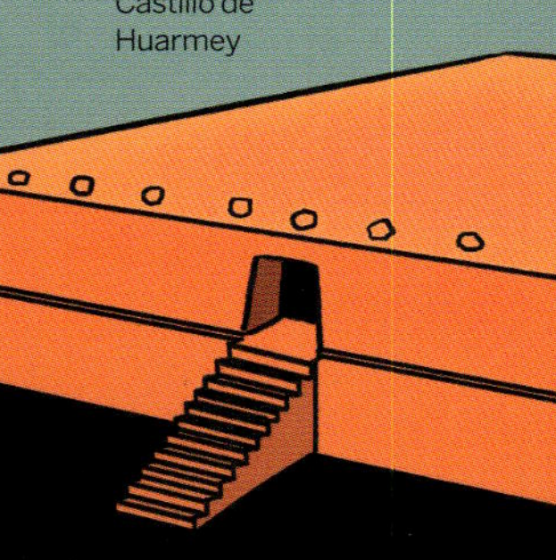

AN UNEXPECTED CLUE
Can you imagine an insect collaborating with you on your research? That's what happened to the team of Peruvian and Polish archaeologists, led by Dr. Milosz Giersz, who found the imperial tomb. While they were excavating in the ceremonial chamber, they saw fly larvae appear. That made them suspect there might be organic matter beneath them. They followed the flies' trail and the rest... is history.

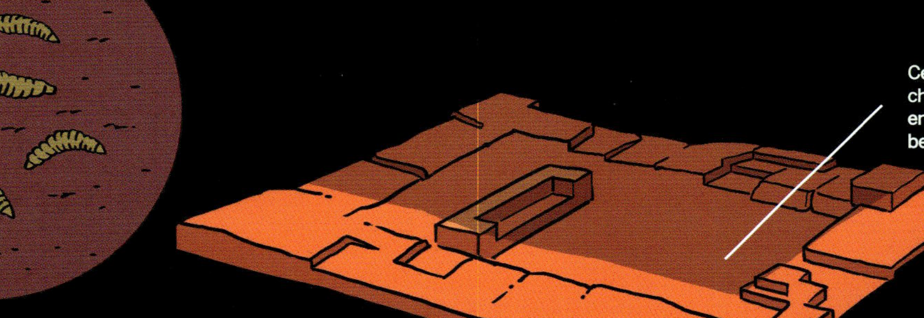

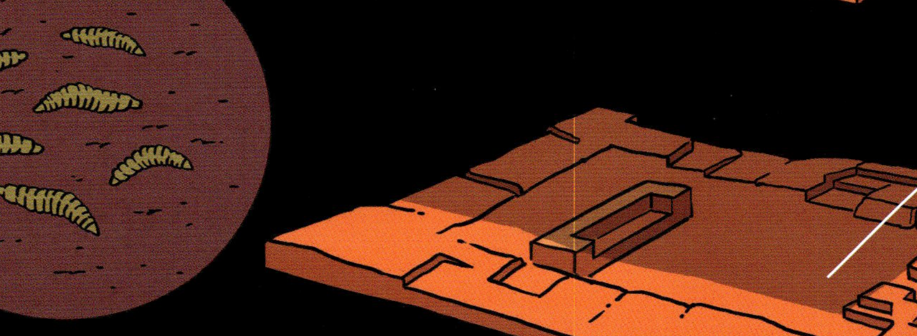

INCREDIBLE EAR ORNAMENTS
Most women in the tomb didn't have as many or as refined objects as the Four Ladies. But, like them, they had incredibly luxurious grave goods, including the beautiful ear ornaments almost all of them wore. Some even had additional pairs stored among their things! More than 100 ear ornaments have been found. They were considered

A WARI POWER CENTER ON THE NORTHERN COAST

CASTILLO DE HUARMEY IS A BUILDING SHAPED LIKE A STEPPED PYRAMID THAT STANDS OUT AGAINST THE LANDSCAPE OF THE VALLEY. IT IS LOCATED JUST OVER A MILE FROM THE CITY OF HUARMEY (ANCASH) AND IS PART OF THE LARGEST WARI COMPLEX ON THE NORTHERN COAST. IT COVERS 110 ACRES, SPANNING MORTUARY AREAS AND THE REMAINS OF MONUMENTAL BUILDINGS. ARCHAEOLOGISTS BELIEVE IT SERVED SEVERAL FUNCTIONS: IN ITS DIFFERENTS SPACES, PUBLIC EVENTS WERE HELD, AND DOMESTIC AND RITUAL ACTIVITIES WERE CARRIED OUT.

* Illustration inspired by Wari pitchers depicting figures holding *Spondylus* shells. **Castillo de Huarmey Archaeological Project.**

WHAT A DISASTER!

IN MAY 1970, AN EARTHQUAKE DAMAGED PART OF THE CASTILLO DE HUARMEY AND EXPOSED SEVERAL TOMBS WITH RICH BURIAL OFFERINGS—TEXTILES, CERAMICS, JEWELRY—THAT HAD REMAINED HIDDEN INSIDE THE ADOBE AND STONE BUILDINGS. FROM THEN ON, LITTLE BY LITTLE, THE SITE WAS DESTROYED BY *HUAQUEROS*. NOT ONLY DID THEY TAKE EVERYTHING THEY FOUND IN THE ANCIENT TOMBS, BUT ALSO THE ADOBE BRICKS, DIRT, AND WOODEN BEAMS THAT WERE USED TO BUILD THIS HISTORIC MONUMENT HUNDREDS OF YEARS AGO.

HUARMEY STYLE

THE CLOTHING AND GRAVE GOODS OF THE WOMEN AT CASTILLO DE HUARMEY GAVE RESEARCHERS INSIGHT INTO HOW THE MOST IMPORTANT WOMEN OF WARI SOCIETY DRESSED. THEY DISCOVERED THAT THEY DRESSED VERY MUCH LIKE THE WOMEN OF THE INCAN NOBILITY DURING THE COLONIAL PERIOD, WHEN THEY WERE TRYING TO IMITATE ANCIENT PERUVIAN QUEENS AND PRINCESSES.

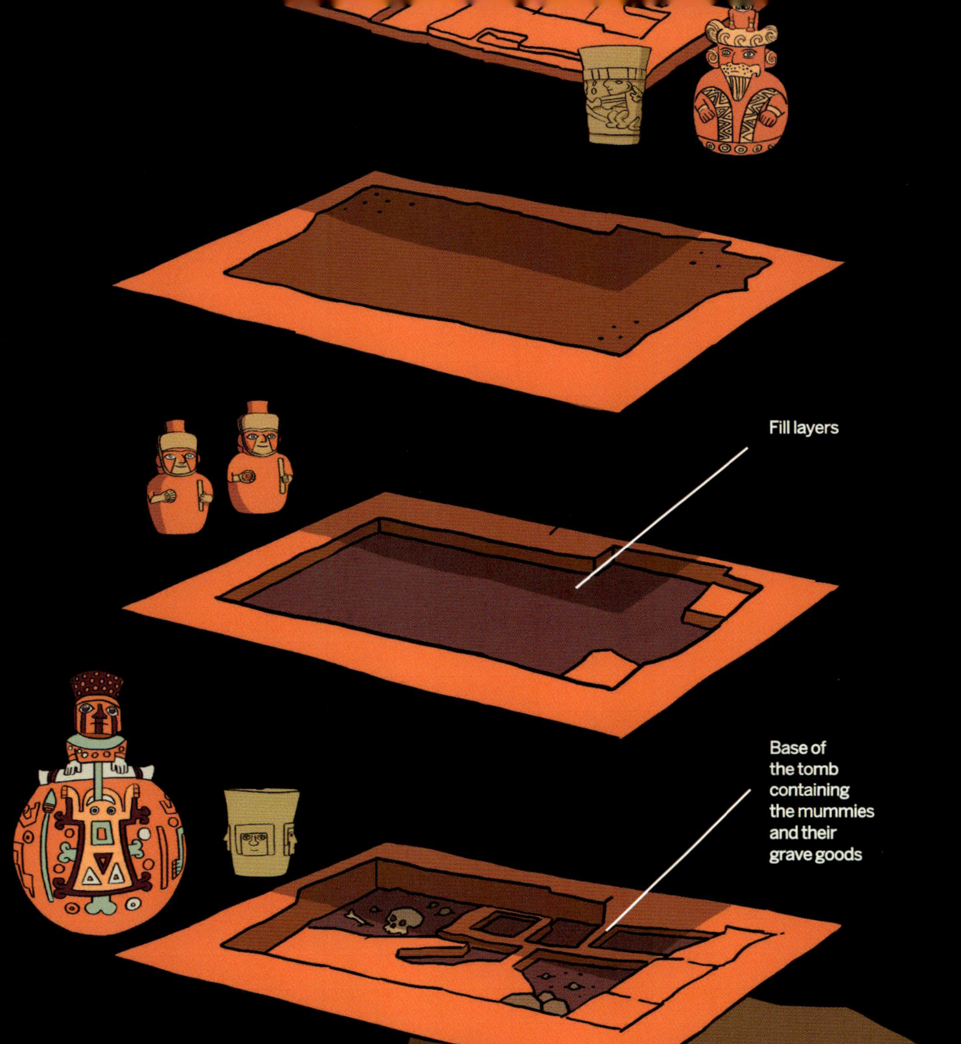

Fill layers

Base of the tomb containing the mummies and their grave goods

* Illustration based on a canteen with polychrome, sculptural decoration of a finely dressed figure seated on a raft (front and back). **Castillo de Huarmey Archaeological Research Project. Peruvian Ministry of Culture.**

THE FOUR LADIES

Four high-status people were found in three rectangular spaces inside the tomb. In the first, there was a woman over 50 years of age next to a young person of about 15 years. In the second was the Principal Lady, who was given this name by researchers because she is the oldest: about 60 years of age. The final space held a middle-aged woman, between 35 and 40 years old. All were placed in the tomb with exceptionally rich and luxurious grave goods.

Principal Lady

THE FOUNDER OF LAMBAYEQUE
We can better understand the lives of the Lambayeque—a society that emerged around the year 800—by looking at the story of Naylamp, their great founder, who was thought to be the ancestor of their powerful leaders. Naylamp wasn't seen as a god but as a wise, brave man who came from the sea, which was fundamental to the economy and belief system of these coastal people.

THE PRIESTESS OF CHORNANCAP
This powerful Lambayeque woman's tomb was found near Huaca Chornancap (Chiclayo). Her body had been placed in the seated position of the funerary bundles, and she was accompanied by seven other women, as well as by rich offerings and remnants of food. On the objects found in the tomb, and also on its walls, there are images of waves and symbols representing the sea and the moon, Andean goddesses associated with feminine power.

LAMBAYEQUE | AD 800–1350

Naylamp's Arrival

Long ago, so long that no one remembers when, the people living on the northern coast spotted a fleet of ships coming from the horizon. In command was Naylamp, a great warrior, accompanied by his wife Ceterni, a court of women, numerous soldiers, and servants.

The first to disembark from the main ship was Pita Zofi, the official trumpeter, who sounded his *Strombus* shell loudly to announce the warrior's arrival. Next came Ñinacola, whose job was caring for the seat and litter on which Naylamp was carried; Ñinavintue, who was in charge of drinks; Fonga Sigde, who sprinkled seashell powder wherever his lord went; Occholalo, the official cook; Xam Muchec, whose job was to paint the warrior's face; Ollopcopoc, who was tasked with bathing him; and Llapchiluli, who was in charge of weaving his clothes and sewing his feather accessories.

Naylamp established his authority on the northern coast of Peru and was a very wise leader. He was able to establish peace among different ethnic groups, developed agriculture and the ceramic industry, and standardized religious practices. Under his leadership, great temples and palaces were built. The most important was the temple of Chot. In its center, a green stone idol called Llampayec, meaning "statue and figure of Naylamp," was placed.

Naylamp's reign was long, and everyone lived in peace and prosperity throughout it. They say that when he died, he became a bird, parted the heavens, and disappeared. From that moment on, the people of the north worshipped him in the form of the Llampayec idol at the temple of Chot. His descendants were great leaders and lords of the kingdom we now call Lambayeque.

* This description was inspired by Miguel Cabello Balboa's 1576 account of an interview with Martin Farrochumbi, the *curaca* (local elder) of Tucume. A later version of the legend of Naylamp was written by Justo Modesto Rubiños y Andrade in 1782 in the towns of Morrope and Pacora (Lambayeque).

ART TO IMPART

THE HISTORY OF THE LAMBAYEQUE KINGDOM, ITS RITUALS, AND ITS SYMBOLS WERE EXPRESSED THROUGH CERAMIC VESSELS, TEXTILES, METAL OBJECTS, BUILDINGS, AND MURALS. FROM ADMINISTRATIVE CENTERS SCATTERED THROUGHOUT THE VALLEYS, THE ELITES CONTROLLED THE WORK OF GOLDSMITHS AND ARTISANS, WHO MADE LUXURY OBJECTS FOR THE ENTIRE REGION. AMONG THEIR BEST-KNOWN PIECES ARE THOSE IN THE STYLE NOW KNOWN AS "*HUACO REY*" (KING *HUACO*): CERAMIC BOTTLES THAT WERE USED IN RITUALS AND MIGHT REPRESENT NAYLAMP.

LAMBAYEQUE *HUACO REY* FOUND IN AN ELITE PERSON'S TOMB IN SAN JOSE DE MORO

ENCHANTING EYES

RESEARCHERS HAVE DESCRIBED THE DISTINCTIVE EYES OF LAMBAYEQUE CHARACTERS IN MANY WAYS. THEY ARE LARGE AND CAN BE SHAPED LIKE ALMONDS OR LIKE OUTSTRETCHED WINGS. ALTHOUGH WE DON'T KNOW WHY THEY HAVE THIS SPECIAL SHAPE, THEY ARE THOUGHT TO REPRESENT NAYLAMP AND, THEREFORE, ALSO LEADERS AND MEMBERS OF THE ELITE.

* Illustration based on a gold Lambayeque mask and headdress. **Museo de Sicán.**

THE SICAN COMPLEX

A group of pyramids and mausoleums rising out of the thick vegetation of the Pomac forest, 20 miles from the city of Chiclayo, Sican was the most important ceremonial center of the Lambayeque kingdom between the years 900 and 1100. It's made up of more than 12 buildings of different sizes and shapes, some built over incredibly deep royal tombs. From here, Lambayeque leaders governed several communities in the nearby valleys (Lambayeque, La Leche, Reque, and Zaña).

* The name of the mythical founder varies in colonial sources, as well as among researchers: Naymlap, Naylamp, Ñaimlap, Ñam-la, or Nam-la. Interestingly, in the Muchik language, *ñain* means "bird" and *la* is "water." Even the figure of the sea bird, present in Lambayeque art, is closely linked to the story of Ñaimlap: according to his kin, when he died he turned into a bird and flew away.

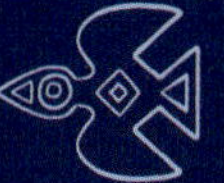

LAMBAYEQUE | AD 800–1350

Chan Chan, a Great City by the Sea

Across from the present-day beach resort town of Huanchaco—famous among surfers for its big waves—sits the centuries-old metropolis of Chan Chan, capital of the ancient Chimu kingdom. Its mud palaces, with their imposing walls, were built over the course of five centuries, between the years 800 and 1350. During that time, Chan Chan grew to an area of nine square miles—larger than any European city of the same era!

Each of its ten palaces, built over the centuries, corresponds to a Chimu ruler. Around them were residences for the elite and neighborhoods of farmers and fishermen, where those who served the great lords lived. These neighborhoods also housed the workshops of artisans, who made metal objects, ceramics, and textiles for the entire kingdom. The rulers organized ceremonies and feasts during which large crowds gathered in the plazas.

Just like today's modern capitals, Chan Chan was very cosmopolitan, bringing together about 70,000 people from different parts of the kingdom. The Chimu borrowed some of their customs and technology from other societies and adapted them according to their tastes and needs (a practice later used by the Incas).

The kingdom's golden age came to an end after a long war against the Incas.

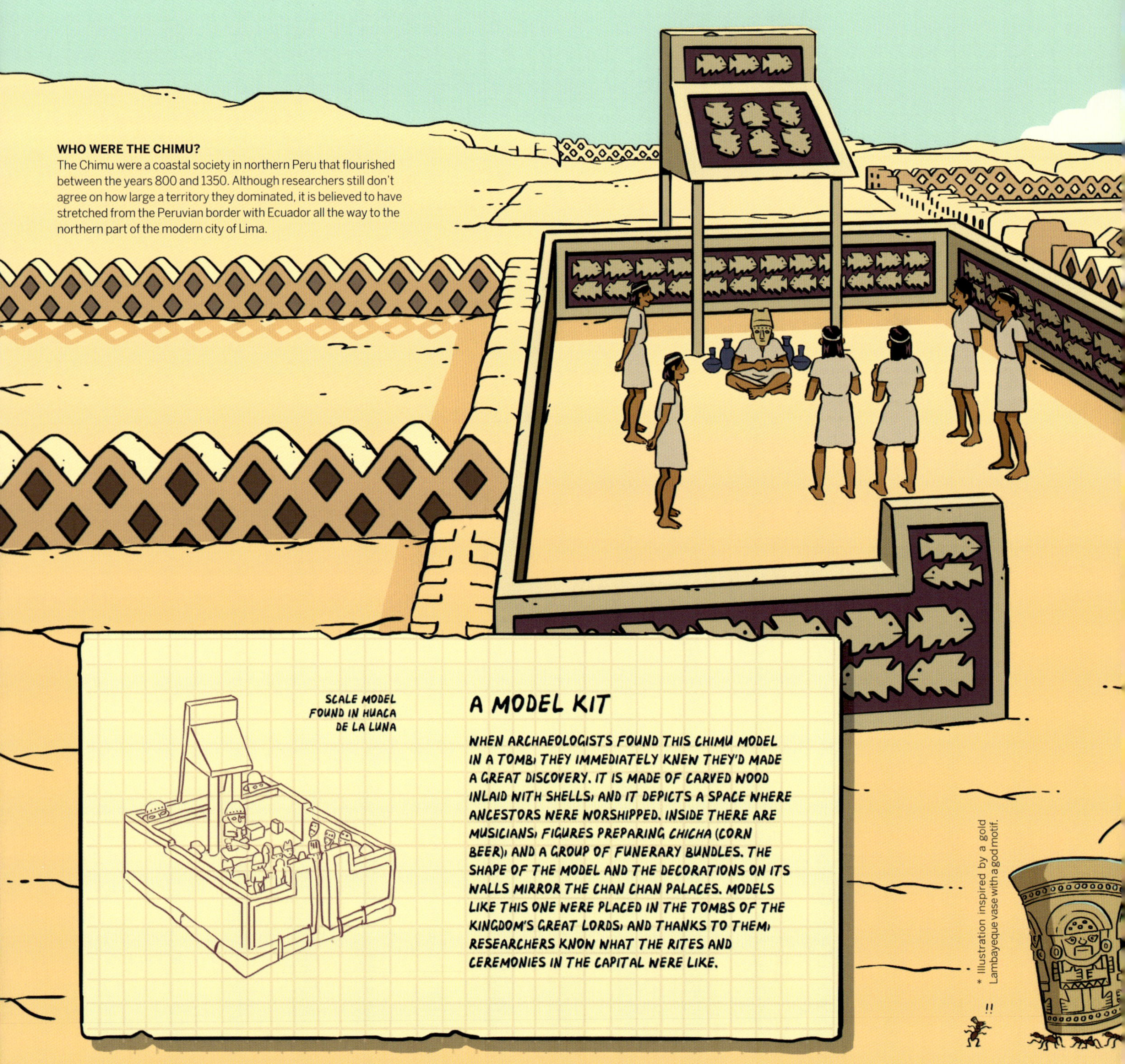

WHO WERE THE CHIMU?
The Chimu were a coastal society in northern Peru that flourished between the years 800 and 1350. Although researchers still don't agree on how large a territory they dominated, it is believed to have stretched from the Peruvian border with Ecuador all the way to the northern part of the modern city of Lima.

SCALE MODEL FOUND IN HUACA DE LA LUNA

A MODEL KIT

WHEN ARCHAEOLOGISTS FOUND THIS CHIMU MODEL IN A TOMB, THEY IMMEDIATELY KNEW THEY'D MADE A GREAT DISCOVERY. IT IS MADE OF CARVED WOOD INLAID WITH SHELLS, AND IT DEPICTS A SPACE WHERE ANCESTORS WERE WORSHIPPED. INSIDE THERE ARE MUSICIANS, FIGURES PREPARING CHICHA (CORN BEER), AND A GROUP OF FUNERARY BUNDLES. THE SHAPE OF THE MODEL AND THE DECORATIONS ON ITS WALLS MIRROR THE CHAN CHAN PALACES. MODELS LIKE THIS ONE WERE PLACED IN THE TOMBS OF THE KINGDOM'S GREAT LORDS, AND THANKS TO THEM, RESEARCHERS KNOW WHAT THE RITES AND CEREMONIES IN THE CAPITAL WERE LIKE.

* Illustration inspired by a gold Lambayeque vase with a god motif.

GAZE LOVINGLY AT THE SEA

LIKE ALL COASTAL PEOPLES, THE CHIMU HAD A VERY SPECIAL RELATIONSHIP WITH THE SEA. THE INTERIOR WALLS OF THE CHAN CHAN PALACES WERE DECORATED WITH MARINE MOTIFS, LIKE WAVES, FISH, COASTAL BIRDS, CRABS, AND LOBSTERS. THEY WERE ALSO DECORATED WITH SCENES OF DAILY LIFE SHOWING FISHERMEN CASTING THEIR NETS INTO THE SEA. THE REEDBEDS WHERE THE CHIMU COLLECTED MATERIALS TO CONSTRUCT THEIR RAFTS—CALLED *CABALLITOS DE TOTORA*—WERE CULTIVATED IN THE SAME CITY, IN AREAS SET ASIDE ESPECIALLY FOR THAT PURPOSE.

CABALLITOS DE TOTORA

LIKE THE MOCHE, THE CHIMU WERE EXPERTS AT BUILDING THESE BOATS, WHICH ARE STILL IN USE TODAY, NOT ONLY FOR FISHING BUT ALSO FOR SURFING THE WAVES. THEY'RE ABOUT 16 FEET LONG AND ARE MADE FROM THE LEAVES AND STEMS OF THE TOTORA REED, A PLANT THAT HAS GROWN FOR THOUSANDS OF YEARS IN THE HUANCHACO REGION. IF YOU VISIT THIS BEAUTIFUL BEACH TOWN, GO SURFING ON A *CABALLITO*!

LIFE´S SWEETER BY THE SEA

The kingdom's fishermen sailed in small reed boats when angling and on big rafts with nets to catch larger quantities of fish. On the beaches, they gathered mollusks, crustaceans, and seaweed. They even went diving to find species in deeper water.

GREAT ARTISANS

Chimu artisans were masters of feather art (clothing and ornaments covered with colorful feathers), wood carving, mat making, and work in shells and semiprecious stones. Many of their most notable metal objects were made by skilled goldsmiths of the Lambayeque kingdom. Their delicate goldwork and fine textiles stand out in particular.

STOLEN TREASURE

In the ceremonies that took place in the temples and plazas of Chan Chan, they used resplendent gold cups and fabulous silver bowls. Unfortunately, the looting that took place after the Spaniards arrived—during the 16th and 18th centuries—has left us only stories about the remarkable treasures that were stolen from the royal mausoleums. Some say there were so many objects made of precious metals that they would amount to three or four times the famous ransom offered by the Inca Atahualpa to Francisco Pizarro: one room full of gold and two of silver.

* Chimu bottle depicting a bird. **Larco Museum. Object code: ML008488.**

A Treasure at the Bottom of the Sea

In the warm, rocky depths of the equatorial sea lives a spiny-shelled mollusk that was a real treasure for the ancient Peruvians: the *Spondylus*. It was known as *mullu*, and it symbolized water and fertility, two fundamental elements for Andean peoples dedicated to cultivating the land. It was used as an offering to the gods and also to create jewelry and ornaments for the most important people in the society.

THE *SPONDYLUS* ROUTE
A long-distance *Spondylus* exchange system began developing with the Moche, and it gradually became a wider and wider network. By the time of the Incas, the *Spondylus* route connected different communities from Manta (Ecuador) to Collao (Bolivia). The shells arrived by sea from Ecuador to the coast of Tumbes, and from there they traveled across the Inca Road or Qhapaq Ñan to all of Tahuantinsuyo.

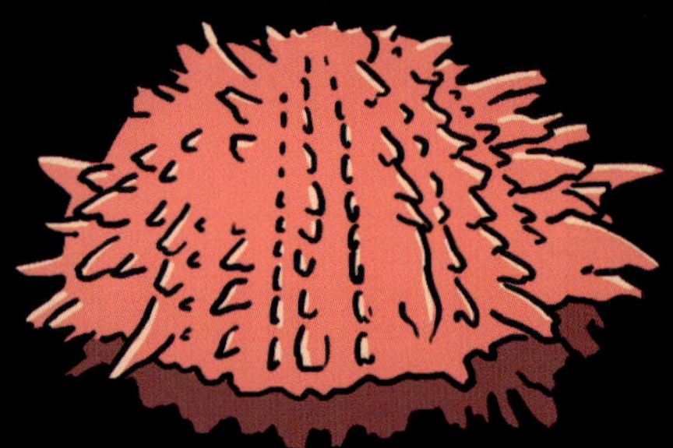

WHAT IS *SPONDYLUS* LIKE?
Its shell has unique colors, ranging from white to orange, red, and purple. It lives in different oceans throughout the world, but the best-known species in South America are *Spondylus princeps* and *Spondylus calcifer*.

ANCESTRAL TREASURES
The use of *Spondylus* in the Andean region is ancient, dating back to the Caral society, the first civilization in the Americas. In the following centuries, it gained importance along with the shells of *Strombus galeatus*, another highly valued species of mollusk, which was used to make trumpets or *pututus*. Both were considered luxury goods and were obtained through trade routes that covered great distances.

FORBIDDEN BY THE INCA
According to the chronicler Garcilaso de la Vega, harvesting *Spondylus* was an extremely dangerous task, so much so that the Incan ruler himself forbade inhabitants of the coast of Tahuantinsuyo from doing it. Only fishermen of the equatorial region, who belonged to societies that traditionally engaged in free diving, were allowed to do so.

THE *STROMBUS* MONSTER
A mythical creature that appears in Moche art, it is protected by a conch shell. It has a snake's head with ears, a feline body, claws, and a long snout with antennae. It doesn't seem very friendly—it's almost always seen fighting against humans.

Incan *paccha* (vessel with a spout) used in fertility rituals and water worship, concepts linked to the sea and its divine fruits, the *Spondylus* shells.

* Illustration based on a paccha with a sculptural *Spondylus* motif. **Museo de Arte de Lima.**

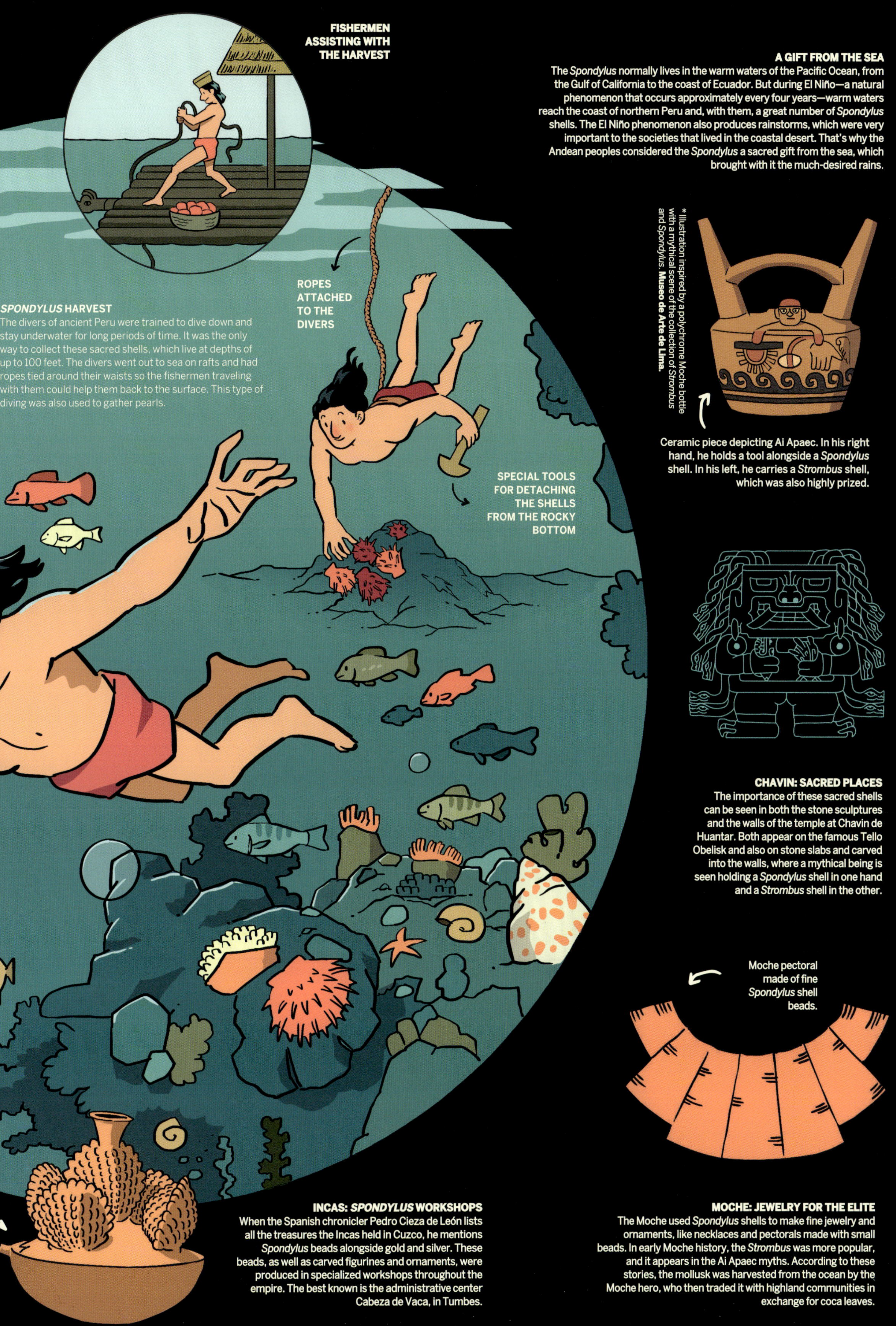

SPONDYLUS HARVEST

The divers of ancient Peru were trained to dive down and stay underwater for long periods of time. It was the only way to collect these sacred shells, which live at depths of up to 100 feet. The divers went out to sea on rafts and had ropes tied around their waists so the fishermen traveling with them could help them back to the surface. This type of diving was also used to gather pearls.

A GIFT FROM THE SEA

The *Spondylus* normally lives in the warm waters of the Pacific Ocean, from the Gulf of California to the coast of Ecuador. But during El Niño—a natural phenomenon that occurs approximately every four years—warm waters reach the coast of northern Peru and, with them, a great number of *Spondylus* shells. The El Niño phenomenon also produces rainstorms, which were very important to the societies that lived in the coastal desert. That's why the Andean peoples considered the *Spondylus* a sacred gift from the sea, which brought with it the much-desired rains.

* Illustration inspired by a polychrome Moche bottle with a mythical scene of the collection of *Strombus* and *Spondylus*. **Museo de Arte de Lima.**

Ceramic piece depicting Ai Apaec. In his right hand, he holds a tool alongside a *Spondylus* shell. In his left, he carries a *Strombus* shell, which was also highly prized.

CHAVIN: SACRED PLACES

The importance of these sacred shells can be seen in both the stone sculptures and the walls of the temple at Chavin de Huantar. Both appear on the famous Tello Obelisk and also on stone slabs and carved into the walls, where a mythical being is seen holding a *Spondylus* shell in one hand and a *Strombus* shell in the other.

Moche pectoral made of fine *Spondylus* shell beads.

INCAS: *SPONDYLUS* WORKSHOPS

When the Spanish chronicler Pedro Cieza de León lists all the treasures the Incas held in Cuzco, he mentions *Spondylus* beads alongside gold and silver. These beads, as well as carved figurines and ornaments, were produced in specialized workshops throughout the empire. The best known is the administrative center Cabeza de Vaca, in Tumbes.

MOCHE: JEWELRY FOR THE ELITE

The Moche used *Spondylus* shells to make fine jewelry and ornaments, like necklaces and pectorals made with small beads. In early Moche history, the *Strombus* was more popular, and it appears in the Ai Apaec myths. According to these stories, the mollusk was harvested from the ocean by the Moche hero, who then traded it with highland communities in exchange for coca leaves.

BETWEEN THE ANDES AND THE JUNGLE
The Chachapoyas lived in the present-day regions of Amazonas and San Martin, between the Huallaga and Marañon Rivers. To one side, their neighbors were the tribal societies of the jungle and, to the other, communities of the Cajamarca society. Their territory included a wide variety of climates and settings, each with their own flora and fauna, from the cold puna (high plateau) to the warm jungle plain.

HOW DID THE CHACHAPOYAS LIVE?
On hilltops and mountain slopes, Chachapoyas communities built both small villages with only a dozen houses and large towns with more than 400. They created terraces to stabilize the land and then built circular buildings on top of them. Some of these settlements—like Kuelap—were protected by high stone walls.

THE MOST BEAUTIFUL
According to the Spanish chronicler Pedro Cieza de León, who met them during the conquest of Peru in the 16th century, the Chachapoyas—both men and women—stood out for their striking good looks and luxurious wool clothing.

KUELAP: THE SEAT OF POWER
Kuelap is the largest of the Chachapoyas settlements and was the center of their political and religious power. It's made up of more than 400 buildings and is believed to have had about 3,000 residents! It's located right in the middle of the cloud forest, at the top of Barreta Hill (Amazonas region), almost 10,000 feet above sea level. It is protected by massive walls that are up to 60 feet high in some places. To get there, you have to go up a passageway lined by high walls, which gets narrower and narrower until only one person can enter. That single entrance guaranteed their protection!

CHACHAPOYAS | AD 900-1470

Lords of the Clouds

Deep in the forest that covers the Peruvian Andes, where the treetops are wrapped in clouds, lived the Chachapoyas. They were organized into family clans or lordships with their own governments, but they made alliances amongst themselves and shared the same customs. Researchers believe they had a very organized military structure because they were also skilled warriors.

From roughly the years 800 to 1535, these "lords of the clouds" stayed mostly isolated, but they were able to conquer a mountainous territory with a very humid climate. They built stepped terraces on the mountainsides, where they grew corn, potatoes, yuca (cassava), beans, and other crops. This allowed them to feed themselves and store provisions for the humid, rainy months.

To protect their ancestors' bodies, the Chachapoyas buried them on rocky mountain slopes. The mummified bodies were wrapped in textiles and placed inside large clay sarcophagi, which were put in hard-to-reach places. They also built mausoleums (buildings or structures for burying the deceased), which were about 10 feet tall and could contain hundreds of mummies.

The history of the Chachapoyas was shrouded in mystery until the mid-19th century, when European explorers found the remains of their cities and fortresses. Today, we know they were fierce rivals of the Incas and resisted the great empire for a long time before being defeated and becoming part of Tahuantinsuyo. Archaeologists continue to research and excavate the most remote sites in the high jungle, hoping to find new clues to understanding the history of this fascinating culture.

GHOST TOWN

Far from the humidity and dense vegetation of the forest, the Chachapoyas built villages into cliff walls, where their mummified ancestors would "live." The rectangular houses were made of stone and had small windows that let in some air and light. Inside these houses, they placed pots, ornaments, food, and other offerings for the ancestors.

Mausoleums of Revash, in Luya Province (Amazonas). Its walls were painted red and could be seen from far away.

A VARIETY OF FOODS

In addition to the vegetables and legumes they harvested, the Chachapoyas ate meat from guinea pigs and camelids—llamas and alpacas—as well as wild forest animals like deer, ducks, turkeys, and doves. Researchers have found that they even ate caiman meat, which they must have gotten through trade with Amazonian tribes.

SKILLED HEALERS

According to ancient Incan and colonial accounts, the Chachapoyas had a reputation as herbalists, healers, and witch doctors. Since they had contact with communities in the Amazon jungle, they had access to medicinal crops and became familiar with the properties of a wide variety of plants and herbs.

SARCOPHAGI OF KARAJIA

THE SARCOPHAGI OF KARAJIA (OR CARAJIA) ARE THE MOST ELABORATE EVER FOUND IN THE REGION OF THE CHACHAPOYAS. RESEARCHERS BELIEVE THIS FORM OF BURIAL IS OLDER THAN THE RECTANGULAR MAUSOLEUMS. THEY WERE MADE USING A MIXTURE OF STONE, CLAY, WOOD, AND REEDS, AND THEY WERE BUILT EXACTLY WHERE THEY STILL STAND: HIGH UP ON CLIFFS AND CRAGS. THE SARCOPHAGI ARE ARRANGED IN ROWS —ONE AGAINST THE OTHER—AND LOOK OUT OVER LAKES OR VALLEYS.

CHANCAY | AD 1000-1400

Master Weavers

Can you imagine breaking ground on a large construction site and finding an old tomb? Yikes! That's what happened at the end of the 19th century to workers building a railroad from Lima to the seaside resort town of Ancon. The construction work revealed an old cemetery that caught the attention of archaeologists. Inside, they found the bodies of men and women from different pre-Hispanic societies—including the Chancay—along with a large quantity of offerings and fabulous textiles.

The Chancay society emerged more than 1,000 years ago in the coastal valley of the same name, further south than their Lambayeque and Chimu neighbors. The Chancay people lived in sprawling villages that had spacious buildings with access ramps, palaces, and workshops. They were great weavers and potters: they created many delicate pieces that continue to captivate both researchers and lovers of art and history.

Chancay weavers mastered the entire range of colors and techniques that were known in their time. They produced fabrics that were embroidered, woven, decorated with feathers and metal objects, painted, and printed. They created fine gauzelike garments made using a unique kind of weave or lace, like a net. They made little dolls out of highly detailed embroidered fabrics, and they designed clothing for their traditional ceramic figurines, called *cuchimilcos*.

In Chancay art, there are no trophy heads or jaguars or battle scenes, so archaeologists assume they were a peaceful people. Nevertheless, between the years 1000 and 1400, their way of life spread throughout the central coast—from the Huaura Valley in the north to the Chillon Valley in the south—and continued on even after the arrival of the Incas.

HOW DID THE CHANCAY LIVE?

The Chancay had a hierarchical society: there were great lords and there were those who served them. Specialized artisans produced luxury objects for the elite, including fine garments, *Spondylus necklaces*, silver cups, and mother-of-pearl earrings, among other things. They were a very industrious people, who dedicated themselves to cultivating the land, fishing, music, pottery, weaving, jewelry making, etc. Their people lived in large villages located around farmland, like the monumental sites at Lauri, Puerto Chancay, and Pisquillo Chico.

INSIDE OUT AND UPSIDE DOWN

The Chancay wove tapestries to make articles of clothing. That's why it was important to meticulously work both sides of the fabric—any movement of the body could reveal the other side! European tapestries, on the other hand, were used to decorate walls or upholster furniture. In those situations, only one side of the fabric was visible, so imperfections on the other side didn't matter as much.

BOW-WOW!

The Peruvian dog, also called a "hairless dog," is one of the favorite motifs in Chancay art. While these dogs appear on Moche ceramics accompanying the hero Ai Apaec on his dangerous adventures or hunting deer, they seem to have had a quieter life in Chancay society.

TEXTILE ART

THE PRINCIPAL MATERIALS USED IN CHANCAY TEXTILES WERE COTTON AND WOOL. LIKE THEIR CERAMICS, THESE WERE PRODUCED IN SPECIALIZED WORKSHOPS. CHANCAY TEXTILES ARE NOTABLE FOR THEIR WIDE VARIETY OF COLORS AND SHADES, AS WELL AS FOR THE DELICACY OF THEIR FAMOUS GAUZE: LACE FABRIC THAT WAS TRANSLUCENT AND LIGHT, YET STIFF, AND WAS WORN AS A HEADDRESS.

FRAGMENT OF CHANCAY GAUZE

WHAT CHARACTERS

Chancay potters depicted a variety of characters on their ceramic pieces: hunters, farmers, and fishermen, among others. Some of the most common are *chinos*, globular pitchers displaying people drinking chicha or making offerings, and *cuchimilcos* or *patones*, human figures with long legs and short, outstretched arms. The latter have been found as offerings in Chancay tombs, always in pairs (man and woman).

SHAPES AND DESIGNS

ON THEIR CLOTH, THE CHANCAY DEPICTED ANIMALS, PLANTS, PEOPLE, MYTHICAL BEINGS, AND SCENES OF DAILY LIFE. MANY OF THESE WERE PAINTED ON PLAIN COTTON FABRIC THAT WORKED LIKE CANVAS. IN CONTRAST, THEIR GAUZE DEPICTS BIRDS, FISH, AND FELINES THAT ARE REPEATED TO FORM PATTERNS. THESE DESIGNS WERE ALSO COPIED ONTO THEIR CERAMICS.

MOLD-MADE PRODUCTION

In their workshops, potters used molds to mass-produce pieces: a single Chancay tomb might contain more than 100 ceramic vessels and figurines! Painted designs were achieved by drawing fine lines in dark violet, which is sometimes mistaken for black. The contrast of this dark paint against the pottery's white background highlights the details in the designs. To achieve this background color, they made their pottery using white clays, like kaolin.

Chancay dolls representing a group of weavers.

Chancay sampler formed by joining several woven scraps. Each one is different, displaying their workshops' designs, arrangements, and techniques.

* Illustration based on a sampler of Chancay fabrics. **Museo de Arte de Lima.**

DOLLS FROM BEYOND THE GRAVE

The Chancay's woven dolls weren't toys: they were placed deep inside tombs, next to the bundles that wrapped the mummified bodies of the deceased. They were made using fabric scraps, rags, sticks wrapped in colored thread, and other accessories. In some cases, archaeologists have found single dolls, but they also appear in groups, in scenes representing moments of daily life. They are very striking and a great source of information, as they show us what their clothing, their hairstyles, and even their make-up were like.

INCA | AD 1400-1532

The Great Incan Empire

In just over 100 years, the Incas forged a great empire that spanned the length of the Andes mountain range, covering almost all of South America, from the jungles of present-day Ecuador to southern Chile and Argentina. It was called Tahuantinsuyo—which means "four regions united"—and it was inhabited by at least six million people from different communities.

To connect all the parts of this immense territory, the Incas built the Qhapaq Ñan: an impressive network of roads snaking through the mountains, which was more than 20,000 miles long. The *chasquis*, or Incan messengers, were in charge of carrying official messages and news across these Andean "highways," which soldiers also traveled to get to their next post. The *chasquis* were so efficient they could carry mail faster than the Spanish horses!

From Cuzco, the capital of Tahuantinsuyo, the highest authority—the Sapa Inca—ruled over all his people. To organize work and production, they used a base-10 control system (i.e., groups of 10). In this way, administrators could supervise very large groups of up to 10,000 families or very small groups of just 10 families.

To keep a meticulous record of all kinds of information, the Incas adapted and perfected the *quipus*, a system of knotted strings created by the Wari (see pages 46–47). Their production, handling, and interpretation were the job of the *quipucamayocs*, who studied from an early age to be able to carry out this important task.

From the beginning of its expansion, around the year 1430, until the arrival of the Spaniards in 1532, Tahuantinsuyo became the most important empire in the Americas. After the downfall and death of its last leader, the Inca Atahualpa, his people continued standing up to the Spanish for 40 more years. And rebellions, large and small, continued taking place throughout the colony.

THE SAPA INCA
Unlike in Europe, the Incan people's highest authority did not inherit power automatically. The Sapa Inca—which in Quechua means "unique Inca"—was elected from among several male candidates belonging to the Cuzco nobility. It's unknown exactly how many there were: some researchers think it's possible that two rulers exercised power at the same time and in a complementary way.

THE INCAN ARMY
In the Andean world, facing an enemy was a sacred ritual. That's why Incan warriors showed respect to their rivals by wearing their most elegant clothes into battle. During the first military campaigns, some groups agreed to ally themselves with the Incas and become part of their army. As a result, their numerous troops were made up of people from different communities.

KNOTS THAT COUNT
Today, there are about 1,000 *quipus* held in different museums and private collections. Of these, 85 percent record numerical information, like tribute payments, how many resources were stored, or a region's total population. The other 15 percent probably hold different kinds of stories, like memoirs, genealogies, poems, or songs.

CHOSEN WOMEN
The *acllas* were women chosen in childhood to live away from their families in a special residence: the *acllawasi*. There, they learned to make the finest-quality wool and textiles, as well as to prepare *chicha*, a fermented corn drink that was very important in Incan rituals.

THE BRIDGES OF THE QHAPAQ ÑAN

The Incas were very skilled at adapting to the diverse territory of the Andes. This can be seen in the different kinds of bridges they built, some of which cross deep chasms. Bridges of rope, wood, and stone were built all along the great Inca Road, according to the resources and conditions of the landscape. One of the most famous is the Queshuachaca suspension bridge, which you can visit in the Canas Province (Cuzco).

AGRICULTURAL TECHNOLOGY

The Incas used different ancestral techniques to take advantage of and improve the quality of the soil. On steep mountain slopes, they built platforms or terraces. In the valleys, they used complex irrigation systems. And in the frozen puna (high plateau), they used sunken fields or *cochas* to increase the soil's moisture, and raised fields or *waru warus* to protect crops from flooding.

ILLUSTRIOUS ANCESTORS

After the rulers' deaths, their bodies were preserved, and their mummies—dressed in luxurious clothing—received very special treatment. They had servants to care for them and were carried in procession during big celebrations. They were even invited to banquets and feasts and would visit different parts of the empire!

POWERFUL MAMACONAS

When the Spaniards arrived in Peru, they were surprised to find hundreds of women in Tahuantinsuyo's main temples, but they didn't understand and couldn't explain what their role was. The *mamaconas* were powerful and well-respected religious officials: they were in charge of managing temples and sanctuaries, caring for the mummies, and educating the *acllas*. These important women developed their mystical powers in the Hatunkancha (or "big place"), which was also the palace of the Inca Topa Inca Yupanqui (Tupac Yupanqui).

THE INCAN LEGACY

THE INCAS HAVE SPARKED THE IMAGINATION AND WONDER OF ANYONE WHO HAS EVER LEARNED ABOUT THEIR HISTORY AND TRADITIONS. TODAY, THEIR MEMORY LIVES ON IN ARCHAEOLOGICAL MONUMENTS THAT HAVE STOOD THE TEST OF TIME AND ARTIFACTS KEPT IN MUSEUMS, BUT ALSO IN TRADITIONS THAT HAVE BEEN REINVENTED AND ARE BEING KEPT ALIVE, SUCH AS THE INTI RAYMI OR FEAST OF THE SUN. THEIR LEGACY CAN ALSO BE SEEN IN PERUVIAN CUISINE—RECOGNIZED AS ONE OF THE WORLD'S MOST DIVERSE AND SOPHISTICATED—AND ALSO IN ART, FASHION, AND POPULAR CULTURE. THEY EVEN APPEAR IN THE NAME OF A VERY FAMOUS PERUVIAN DRINK: INCA KOLA.

INCA | AD 1400-1532

The Incas' Royal Estates

Did you know Machu Picchu was one of the Inca Pachacuti's royal estates? The estates built by the Incan rulers were big, beautiful residences, and their grounds encompassed palaces, farmland, lakes, and even recreational areas for the nobility. They were built in strategic locations that held great importance for local populations and were ideal places for gathering various resources, like corn, chili pepper, coca, salt, gold, and wood. Entire villages came to work on the estates in order to meet all the needs of the Inca and his family.

THE EMPIRE IN MINIATURE
Some of the work on the estates was done by people who were brought there from distant corners of the empire to oversee farming and other activities. Both they and their descendants would remain in service to the estate owner, and their work would be supervised by the Cuzco nobility. These royal estates were like tiny models of Tahuantinsuyo, where the Incas held power over other populations.

Machu Picchu: Between Heaven and Earth

During the rainy season—between March and October—Machu Picchu appears to be floating amidst clouds that engulf the mountains and drape this ancient city in a shroud of mystery. Its incredible stone buildings are located 8,000 feet above sea level, on a rock ledge between the hills of Huayna Picchu and Machu Picchu. It is located between the Andes and the Amazon, in an area of rugged, steep, and forested terrain that took the Inca Pachacuti great effort to conquer for the empire. To secure his victory, the ruler ordered the construction of this magnificent estate, which today is one of the biggest tourist attractions in the world.

Caquia Xaquixahuana

They say the Inca Huiracocha was the only one to ever live continuously at this estate, which is located on top of a mountain. Although their estates and palaces were comfortable and luxurious, the rulers spent little time in them. They were meant to be permanent residences for their mummies.

PRINCIPAL RULERS AND THEIR ESTATES

- HUIRACOCHA
- PACHACUTI
- TOPA INCA YUPANQUI (TUPAC YUPANQUI)
- HUAYNA CAPAC
- HUASCAR

HUIRACOCHA
Period of Government: until c. 1438
Panaca: Socso *Ayllu*
Estate: Caquia Xaquixahuana

PACHACUTI
Period of Government: c. 1438–14
Panaca: Iñaca Panaca
Estates: Pisac, Ollantaytambo, ar
Machu Picchu

Ollantaytambo

In the early years of Incan expansion, estates were built to commemorate their triumph over certain groups and to solidify the empire's power. For example, an enemy ruler's sons, who were captured by Pachacuti after a difficult battle, participated in the construction of Ollantaytambo.

POWERFUL FAMILIES

FAMILIES DESCENDED FROM PAST INCAN RULERS MADE UP THE NOBILITY OF CUZCO AND WERE KNOWN AS PANACAS. WHEN A RULER DIED, HIS PANACA WAS NO LONGER THE MOST POWERFUL, BUT THEY WOULD STILL HAVE AN IMPORTANT SOCIAL POSITION AS LONG AS THEY WORSHIPPED HIS MUMMY—WHICH CONTINUED TO "LIVE" IN HIS PALACE. EACH INCAN RULER WAS OBLIGED TO ESTABLISH A PANACA AND BUILD AN ESTATE, WHICH WOULD BE OWNED BY HIS FAMILY FOREVER.

Yucay

No obstacle stood in the way of building these magnificent estates. During construction of his residence in the Yucay Valley, the Inca Huayna Capac had the river diverted to the south, on the Cuzco side. He also leveled the hills along the course of the river to create flatlands where food could be grown.

Chinchero

According to the Spanish chronicler Juan de Betanzos, the Topa Inca Yupanqui (Tupac Yupanqui) recruited workers from all over the empire to build this estate. He ordered his men to gather chiefs and their people from throughout his domain and bring them to the city of Cuzco. They were able to bring together no fewer than 20,000 people—a monumental task!

'A INCA YUPANQUI
PAC YUPANQUI)
od of Government: c. 1476–1495
aca: Capac *Ayllu*
te: Chinchero

HUAYNA CAPAC
Period of Government: c. 1498–1527
Panaca: Tomebamba Panaca
Estate: Yucay

HUASCAR
Period of Government: c. 1528–1532
Panaca: Huascar Panaca
Estate: Muina and Calca

Discover Ancient Peru!

Caral

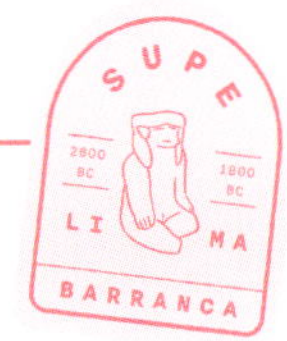

1 CARAL [SEE PAGES 18–19]
You can take a car or a bus to this magnificent citadel, located at kilometer 184 of the Panamericana Norte (at which point, you take a turnoff). Tickets are sold on site, and you can also schedule a guided tour.

Chavin

2A KUNTUR WASI [SEE PAGES 20–21]
This spectacular archaeological complex is located in the province of San Pablo, 42 miles from the city of Cajamarca. You can walk around the site, and you can also visit the Kuntur Wasi Museum, on La Copa hill, to see their beautiful goldwork and ceramic pieces.

2B CHAVIN DE HUANTAR [SEE PAGES 20–25]
Located in the Huari province, in Ancash, the archaeological site at Chavin de Huantar is one of the most iconic places in Peru. There you can see the incredible Lanzon gallery. We recommend that you also visit the National Museum of Chavin, where you will find the Tello Obelisk and several tenon heads.

2C RAIMONDI STELE [SEE PAGES 22–23]
This emblematic piece of Chavin art is currently housed in the National Museum of Archaeology, Anthropology, and History of Peru, in the Pueblo Libre District in Lima.

Paracas

3 PARACAS [SEE PAGES 26–29]
We recommend a visit to the Julio C. Tello Paracas Site Museum (redesigned by architects Sandra Barclay and Jean Pierre Crousse and awarded "Best New Museum in Latin America" in 2018 by the Leading Culture Destinations Awards) and the Adolfo Bermudez Jenkins Regional Museum of Ica, both located in the Ica region.

You can also see Paracas textiles at the Museum of Archaeology and Anthropology at the Universidad Nacional Mayor de San Marcos and at the National Museum of Archaeology, Anthropology, and History of Peru, both in the city of Lima.

Nazca

4 NAZCA [SEE PAGES 30–35]
To learn more about this legendary culture, we recommend that you visit the ancient city of Cahuachi, located in the Nazca District, in the province of the same name, in the Ica region. You can also fly over the Nazca lines.

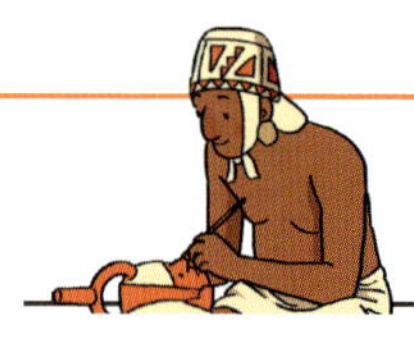

Moche

5 MOCHE [SEE PAGES 36–41]
Huaca del Sol and Huaca de la Luna are located just 15 minutes away from the city of Trujillo, in the region of La Libertad. Take full advantage of your visit by going to the Huacas de Moche Museum and touring the interior of Huaca de la Luna.

Wari

6A WARI AND TIAHUANACO [SEE PAGES 42–43]
To learn more about the Wari and the Tiahuanaco, visit the archaeological sites and museums dedicated to preserving their legacy. Archaeological sites: the Wari and Conchopata archaeological complexes, in Ayacucho; Piquillacta and Espiritu Pampa, in Cuzco; Cerro Baul, in Moquegua; Huiracochapampa, in La Libertad; and Tiahuanaco, in La Paz (Bolivia). Museums: Chiribaya—El Algarrobal, in Moquegua; Carlos Dreyer, in Puno; Tiahuanaco Site Museum, in La Paz (Bolivia); Hipolito Unanue Regional Museum, in Ayacucho; Museo de Arte de Lima and the Larco Museum, both in Lima.

6B CASTILLO DE HUARMEY [SEE PAGES 48–49]
You can also visit the Castillo de Huarmey archaeological site, which is located just half a mile from the city of Huarmey, in the Ancash region. During your visit, you can walk around the complex to learn about its different spaces, and you can also see where the imperial tomb was found.

Lambayeque

7 LAMBAYEQUE [SEE PAGES 50–53]
To learn more about the Lambayeque —also called the Sican—visit the Bosque de Pomac Historic Sanctuary and the pyramids and huacas of the Sican Archaeological Complex (Batan Grande). You can also visit the Chotuna-Chornancap Archaeological Complex and its site museum, all just a few miles away from the city of Chiclayo, in Lambayeque.

MUSEO DE ARTE DE LIMA – MALI. Discover these representative pieces from Peru's ancient cultures, which you've learned about in this book, at the MALI.

Cupisnique

Nazca

Nazca

Nazca

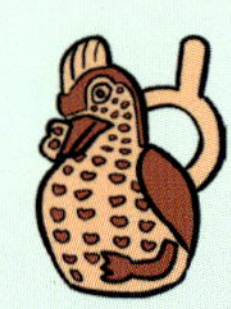
Moche

Moche

Moche

Wari

Chancay

Chancay

Inca

Chachapoyas

8 KUELAP [SEE PAGE 56–57]
You can visit the Kuelap Archaeological Complex (Luya province), the Leymebamba Museum (Chachapoyas province), and the sarcophagi of Karajia (30 miles from the city of Chachapoyas), all in the Amazonas region. In the San Martin region, you can visit the site of Vira Vira, in the Abiseo River National Park.

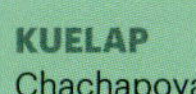

KUELAP
Chachapoyas

KUNTUR WASI
Chavin

CHAN CHAN
Chimu

Inca

11 INCA [SEE PAGES 60–63]
We recommend an immersive trip to the Cuzco region, where you can visit the royal palaces of the Incas, such as Machu Picchu, Chinchero, Yucay, Tipon, Ollantaytambo, and Pisac, among others.

CASTILLO DE HUARMEY
Wari

MACHU PICCHU
Inca

TUMBES
PIURA
LAMBAYEQUE
AMAZONAS
CAJAMARCA
LORETO
SAN MARTIN
LA LIBERTAD
ANCASH
HUANUCO
UCAYALI
PASCO
LIMA
JUNIN
HUANCAVELICA
CUZCO
ICA
AYACUCHO
APURIMAC
PUNO
AREQUIPA
LAKE TITICACA
MOQUEGUA
TACNA

Chimu

9 CHAN CHAN [SEE PAGES 52–53]
In 1986, the pre-Columbian city of Chan Chan was declared a World Heritage Site by UNESCO (United Nations Educational, Scientific and Cultural Organization). It is located just 20 minutes from the city of Trujillo, in La Libertad, and it has a site museum where you can learn more about the Chimu society.

PARACAS SITE MUSEUM
Paracas

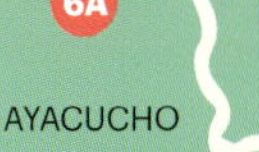

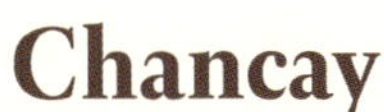

Chancay

10 CHANCAY [SEE PAGES 58–59]
To learn more about the Chancay society and its beautiful textiles, visit the Amano Museum of Pre-Columbian Textiles in the Miraflores District (Lima), as well as the Chancay Municipal Museum in the Chancay District (Huaral).

NAZCA LINES
Nazca

Glossary

We've gathered some words here to help you better understand what they mean and how they´re used in this book. Some come from the pre-Hispanic world, some are in the Quechua language, and some are part of a more complex vocabulary.

Achiote—Plant native to the Americas, also known as annatto. A natural reddish-yellow pigment is extracted from its seeds and has been used since pre-Hispanic times. It also has medicinal properties and is used as a seasoning in food.

Aclla—Women chosen in childhood to live in a special residence, where they would learn to make the finest textiles and to prepare *chicha*, the ritual drink of the Incan Empire.

Acllawasi—Residence where the *acllas* lived.

Antara—Wind instrument, also known as zampoña, siku, or Andean pan flute. Musicians in ancient Peru played it during ceremonies and rituals.

Apu—Spirit in the shape of a mountain, which has the power to protect and care for people or to act as a border between different territories.

Ayllu—Lineage or family group who thought of themselves as descendents of a common ancestor.

Cañan—Small lizard that lives along the northern coast of Peru and was part of the Moche diet. Also known as the Peru desert tegu.

Chicha—Drink prepared with fermented corn, which was used during festivals and rituals. Today, it is also used as an ingredient in Peruvian cuisine.

Chronology—Timeline showing a set of historical events arranged according to the dates when they occurred.

Cocha—In Quechua, cocha means "lagoon." This name also refers to the agricultural technology in which small oases or sunken farms are created to take advantage of the water in the subsoil. In some regions they are called wachaques.

Custard apple—Fruit native to the Andes Mountains, which has a sweet flavor and white pulp with black seeds, also known as cherimoya.

Ecosystem—Ecological system made up of an environment and all its living inhabitants, as well as the relationships among them.

Funerary bundle—Mummified body wrapped in several layers of cloth, containing offerings like vessels, necklaces, or musical instruments.

Hatunkancha—Special place where the *mamaconas* developed their mystical powers. It was located between the Awkaypata plaza and Coricancha, in the city of Cuzco.

Huaca—Sacred person, place, or thing—for example, mummies, sanctuaries, temples, idols, etc.

Huaco—Ceramic objects or vessels found in the *huacas*.

Huaquero—Thief who searches for hidden treasure in the *huacas* and carries out illegal excavations.

Kaolin—Clay that, when fired, produces ceramics in light tones, such as white. It is only found in places with a lot of rain, like the Peruvian jungle and sierra.

Mamacona—Powerful and respected religious official during the Incan Empire. The *mamaconas* were in charge of the administration of temples, the care of mummies, and the education of acllas.

Mausoleum—Very ornate or luxurious tomb, usually of a large size.

Oca—Yellow root with a sweet flavor, native to the Andes.

Offerings—Objects of great value (such as fine textiles, ornaments, vessels, or seashells) that were given as gifts to the *huacas* and priests to ask for the favor of the gods.

Pacay—Long green plant native to the Americas, which produces an edible fruit covered by a soft film that looks like cotton. Also known as ice-cream bean.

Pachaca—Pre-Hispanic settlement or village that was under the authority of a leader or an official.

Panacas—Powerful families, descendants of the Incas who had ruled the empire in the past. They made up the nobility of Cuzco.

Puquio—Spring of water that is part of a system of aqueducts built by the ancient societies of the Peruvian coast.

Pututu—Trumpet made by trimming one of the edges off the shell of the *Strombus* snail.

Quipu— System of cords and knots used by the Incas to record information of all kinds. The first *quipus* were developed by the Wari society.

San Pedro—Variety of cactus used to prepare a hallucinogenic substance and given as an offering during religious rites and ceremonies.

Sepulchre—Tomb, burial place.

Shaman—Priest of ancient Peru whose knowledge was very important to his people. He could interpret the position of the stars and the signs of nature.

Spondylus—Spiny-shelled mollusk that was sacred to the ancient Peruvians. Known as *mullu*, it was a symbol of water and fertility.

Strombus—Marine snail whose shell was highly prized by the ancient Peruvians and was used to make trumpets or *pututus*.

Totora—Plant that has grown in the northern Peruvian region for thousands of years. Its stems and leaves are used to make light boats known as *caballitos de totora*.

Ullucu—Tuber native to the Americas that has been cultivated in Peru for thousands of years.

Uncu—Men's garment, similar to a shirt, worn by the inhabitants of ancient Peru—and also by some mummies!

Waru waru—Earthen platform that's like a floating bed surrounded by water, where crops are planted. The water around the *waru waru* creates a microclimate that helps reduce the effect of frost in the coldest regions of the Andes.

Bibliography

1. Bacha, A. B., & Llanos, D. (2013). ¿Hacia un urbanismo paracas en Ánimas Altas / Ánimas Bajas (valle de Ica)? *Boletín de Arqueología PUCP,* (17), 169–204.
2. Bawden, G. (1996). *The Moche.* Oxford: Blackwell Publishers.
3. Blower, D. (2000). The many facets of mullu: More than just a *Spondylus* shell. *Andean Past, 6*, 209–228.
4. Bourget, S. (2001). Rituals of sacrifice: Its practice at Huaca de la Luna and its representation in Moche iconography. *Studies in the History of Art, 63*, 88–109. http://www.jstor.org/stable/42622316
5. Carmichael, P. (2017). *Evidencia iconográfica de la génesis nasca. Nasca*. Lima y Zúrich: Asociación Museo de Arte de Lima, Museo Rietberg.
6. Castillo, J. L., & Pardo, C. (2009). *De Cupisnique a los incas: el arte del valle de Jequetepeque*. Lima: Museo de Arte de Lima (MALI).
7. Colomer, L. (scriptwriter and host). (May 2021). Cahuachi, la gran ciudad milenaria del sur de Perú [Podcast episode]. *Desenterrando el pasado*. National Geographic. https://open.spotify.com/episode/4kyWEsRlUuZObCe5qYCCfx?si=JOXrFh7ZRpa2upFfEZ678g
8. Cooper, J., & Pardo, C. (2021). *Peru: A journey in time.* London: British Museum.
9. Cornejo, L., & Aguirre, C. S. (2005). *Chimú: laberintos de un traje sagrado.* Museo Chileno de Arte Precolombino.
10. Cortéz, V. (2020). Arte chancay: reconstrucción ritual del mundo. In *Líneas Generales*, (3–4), 8–25. Universidad de Lima.
11. Crousse, J. P., & Cuadra, M. (2021). *Agujeros negros urbanos*. Lima: Patronato Cultural del Perú.
12. Daggett, R. E. (1994). The Paracas mummy bundles of the great necropolis of Wari Kayan: A history. *Andean Past, 4*(1), 7.
13. De la Cruz, M. P. (2013). Templo de la muerte. Imperio wari. *NEO, Suplemento de innovación, tecnología e investigación del semanario puntoedu* (PUCP), 5(61). Lima: Pontificia Universidad Católica del Perú (PUCP).
14. Del Busto Duthurburu, J. A. (Ed.). (2006). *Historia cronológica del Perú*. Lima: Departamento de Relaciones Corporativas de Petróleos del Perú (Petroperú).
15. Dieulafait, F., & Audouin, L. (2017). *Copain de l'archéologie: le guide des explorateurs du temps*. Milan.
16. Frame, M. (2007). Las prendas bordadas de la necrópolis de Wari Kayán. In E. León, (Ed.), *Hilos del pasado. El aporte francés al legado paracas*. Lima: Instituto Nacional de Cultura.
17. Fux, P. (2015). *Chavín*. Lima: Museo de Arte de Lima (MALI).
18. Fux, P., & Pardo, C. (2017). *Nasca*. Lima: Museo de Arte de Lima (MALI).
19. Gänger, S. (2014). *Relics of the past. The collecting and study of Pre-Columbian Antiquities in Peru and Chile, 1837–1911* . Oxford University Press.
20. Giersz, M. (2017). *Castillo de Huarmey. Un centro imperial wari en la costa norte del Perú*. Lima: Ediciones del Hipocampo.
21. Giersz, M., & Pardo C. (2014). *Castillo de Huarmey. El mausoleo imperial wari*. Lima: Museo de Arte de Lima (MALI).
22. Guerrero, R. (Ed.). (2015). *Chachapoyas y Cajamarca en la selva y sierra norte.* Culturas antiguas del Perú (vol. 9). Lima: Editorial Septiembre.
23. Guerrero, R. (Ed.). (2015). *Chavín, un gran centro ceremonial andino*. Culturas antiguas del Perú (vol. 2). Lima: Editorial Septiembre.
24. Guerrero, R. (Ed.). (2015). *Inca, la cumbre de la civilización andina*. Culturas antiguas del Perú (vol. 10). Lima: Editorial Septiembre.
25. Guerrero, R. (Ed.). (2015). *Lambayeque y Chimú, los grandes estados norteños*. Culturas antiguas del Perú (vol. 8). Lima: Editorial Septiembre.
26. Guerrero, R. (Ed.). (2015). *Lima, desarrollo social en la costa central*. Culturas antiguas del Perú (vol. 5). Lima: Editorial Septiembre.
27. Guerrero, R. (Ed.). (2015). *Mochica, desarrollo cultural en la costa norte*. Culturas antiguas del Perú (vol. 3). Lima: Editorial Septiembre.
28. Guerrero, R. (Ed.). (2015). *Nasca, continuidad de la tradición de la costa sur*. Culturas antiguas del Perú (vol. 6). Lima: Editorial Septiembre.
29. Guerrero, R. (Ed.). (2015). *Paracas, desarrollo social en la costa sur*. Culturas antiguas del Perú (vol. 4). Lima: Editorial Septiembre.
30. Guerrero, R. (Ed.). (2015). *Wari, el gran imperio andino y la cultura tiahuanaco*. Culturas antiguas del Perú (vol. 7). Lima: Editorial Septiembre.
31. Hall, S. (2010). Las líneas de Nasca revelan sus secretos. *National Geographic, 26*(3), 2–25.
32. Holmquist, U., & De los Heros, J. A. B. (2010). *El Perú antiguo II (200 a. C. – 500). El periodo de los desarrollos regionales*. Historia del Perú. Lima: Empresa Editora El Comercio.
33. Jennings, J., & Álvarez, W. Y. (Eds.). (2012). *¿Wari en Arequipa?: análisis de los contextos funerarios de La Real.* Museo Arqueológico José María Morante, Universidad Nacional de San Agustín de Arequipa.
34. Jiménez, A. (1982). Introducción a la cultura chancay. In *Chancay*. Colección Arte y tesoros del Perú. Lima: Banco de Crédito del Perú (BCP).
35. Kauffman Doig, F. (2013). *Los chachapoyas.* Lima: Banco de Crédito del Perú (BCP).
36. Kauffmann Doig, F. (1983). *El Perú antiguo.* Historia general de los peruanos, vol. I. Lima: Editorial Peisa.

37. Kaulicke, P. (Ed.). (2000). El periodo arcaico en el Perú: hacia una definición de los orígenes. *Boletín de Arqueología PUCP, 3*. Pontificia Universidad Católica del Perú, Fondo Editorial.
38. Kaulicke, P. (2008). Espacio y tiempo en el Periodo Formativo: una introducción. *Boletín de Arqueología PUCP*, (12), 9–23.
39. Kaulicke, P. (2009). Espacio y tiempo en el Periodo Formativo: algunas reflexiones finales. *Boletín de Arqueología PUCP*, (13), 373–387.
40. Kaulicke, P. (2010). *El Perú antiguo I (9000 a. C. – 200 d. C.). Los periodos arcaico y formativo.* Historia del Perú. Lima: Empresa Editora El Comercio.
41. Kusunoki, R., Pardo, C., & Rucabado, J. (2023). *Los incas.* Lima: Museo de Arte de Lima (MALI).
42. López Cuevas, F. (2005). El *Spondylus* en el Perú prehispánico. Su significación religiosa y económica. *Ámbitos*, (14), 33–42. Córdoba: Asociación de Estudios de Ciencias Sociales y Humanidades.
43. Lumbreras, L. (2007). Apuntes sobre Julio C. Tello, el Maestro. In *Julio C. Tello* (pp. 5–28). Lima: Centro Cultural San Marcos, Museo de Arqueología y Antropología de la UNMSM.
44. Lumbreras, L. G., Carré, E. G., & Del Águila, C. (2005). *Arqueología y sociedad.* Instituto de Estudios Peruanos.
45. Makowski, K. (2004). *Primeras civilizaciones.* Enciclopedia Temática del Perú, vol. IX. Lima: Empresa Editora El Comercio.
46. Mauricio, A. C., Prieto, G., & Pardo, C. (2014). Avances en la arqueología de la cultura Lima. *Boletín de Arqueología PUCP*, (18), 5–14.
47. Moseley, M. E. (1992). *The Incas and their ancestors: The archaeology of Peru*.
48. Museum Rietberg (April 8, 2014). Chavín, el enigmático templo de los Andes peruanos [Video]. *YouTube.* https://youtu.be/ysvTZZVdfQI?si=x-fYbs8wiqUHQ14ke
49. Nair, S., & Protzen J. (2019). Arquitectura y paisaje inca: variación, tecnología y simbolismo. In I. Shimada (Ed.), *El imperio inka* (pp. 357–384). Lima: Fondo Editorial PUCP.
50. Niles, S. (2019). Considerando las fincas reales de los incas: arquitectura, economía, historia. In I. Shimada (ed.), *El imperio inka* (pp. 385–406). Lima: Fondo Editorial PUCP.
51. Pillsbury, J. (2001). *Moche art and archaeology in ancient Peru*. Washington D. C.: National Gallery of Art.
52. Pozzi-Escot, D. (2010). *El Perú antiguo III (500–1400). El Horizonte Medio y los Estados regionales*. Historia del Perú. Lima: Empresa Editora El Comercio.
53. Quebedo, L., & Rubio, M. J. (hosts). (June 2023). El misterio de los chachapoyas, "los guerreros de las nubes" [Podcast episode]. In Despierta tu curiosidad. National Geographic. https://open.spotify.com/episode/5nCdwX-tiopRUbCh8jUu5Us?si=ZTkkDblyQ_6sz19yfvjmXg
54. Reid, W. (1982). Los tejidos Chancay. In Chancay. Colección Arte y tesoros del Perú. Lima: Banco de Crédito del Perú (BCP).
55. Renfrew, C., & Bahn, P. (2012). Archaeology: Theories, methods and practice. Thames and Hudson.
56. Rostworowski, M. (1992). Historia del Tahuantinsuyo. Lima: Instituto de Estudios Peruanos (IEP).
57. Rucabado, J., & Pardo, C. (2016). Moche y sus vecinos, reconstruyendo identidades. Lima: Museo de Arte de Lima (MALI).
58. Shady, R. (2006). La civilización caral. Boletín de Arqueología PUCP, 10, 59–88. Lima: Pontificia Universidad Católica del Perú (PUCP).
59. Shimada, I. (2020). El imperio inka. Fondo Editorial de la PUCP.
60. Solís, R. S. (2006). Caral, Supe: La civilización más antigua de América. Lima: Instituto Nacional de Cultura.
61. Uceda, S., & Mujica, E. (1994). Moche: propuestas y perspectivas (vol. 79). Universidad Nacional de La Libertad.
62. Uceda, S., Morales, R., & Mujica, E. (2016). Huaca de la Luna: templos y dioses moches. WM, World Monuments Fund Perú.
63. Vega Centeno, R., & Vergara, T. (2023). La leyenda de Naylamp en la memoria y la identidad de los pueblos de Lambayeque, costa norte del Perú. Diálogo Andino, (71), 131–144.
64. Velarde, M. I., & De la Mata, P. C. (2018). Transición Paracas-Nasca, continuidad e innovación en los metales. Boletín de Arqueología PUCP, (25), 135–145.

ACKNOWLEDGMENTS

We are grateful to the Larco Museum for allowing us to be inspired by their magnificent pre-Columbian collection, and we appreciate the invaluable work they do to spread knowledge of, and appreciation for, pre-Columbian Peru. We extend our thanks to all the museums in Peru, whose collections were inspiration for many of this book's illustrations.